Contents

2 The Creative Spirit

Teen Novels and Short Stories, Fantasy, Humor, Mystery and Suspense, Poetry, the Arts...

14 Science

Animals, Mind and Body, Brain Food, Ancient Stones and Bones, Planet Earth...

18 Here and Now

Love and Sex, Getting it Together, Overcoming Odds, LGBTQ: Being Gay, War and Peace, Remarkable People, Memoir....

27 One World

Native Americans, Latinos, Black America, Other Countries...

36 Action and Adventure

Do-It-Yourself, Sports, True Adventure...

W9-CSN-017

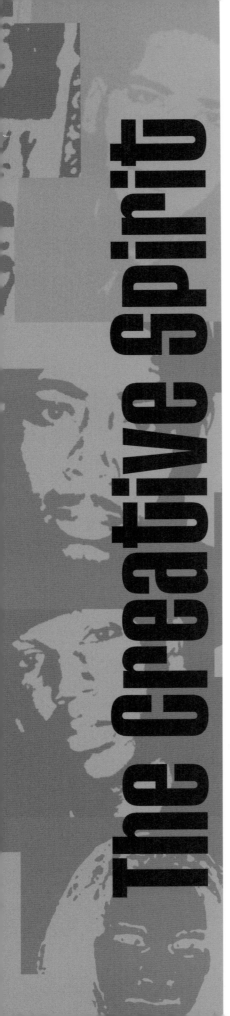

The Creative Spirit

Humor

ANONYMOUS AS TOLD TO TUCKER SHAW
Confessions of a Backup Dancer
Simon Pulse
A crazy summer around a pop diva

CHARLES S. ANDERSON DESIGN COMPANY AND MICHAEL J. NELSON
Happy Kitty Bunny Pony
Abrams
Vintage cute: precious or nauseating

CIRRONE, DORIAN
Dancing in Red Shoes Will Kill You
HarperCollins
Generously busted, genuinely stressed

EHRENHAFT, DANIEL
10 Things to Do Before I Die
Delacorte
Ted, making the most of his last 24 hours

GRANT, VICKI
Quid Pro Quo
Orca
Semi-slacker Cyril solves the case

HIAASEN, CARL
Flush
Knopf
A dip in the ocean; swimming in the toilet

HURSTON, ZORA NEALE AND CHRISTOPHER MYERS
Lies and Other Tall Tales
HarperCollins
Short, wild, wicked stories

KEMP, KRISTEN
The Dating Diaries
Push
Making up for lost time after a break-up

LUBAR, DAVID
Dunk
Clarion
The twisted world of a wisecracking clown

MCGRUDER, AARON
Right to Be Hostile
Three Rivers
Boondocks comics, poking fun at everyone

PEREL, DAVID AND THE EDITORS OF THE WEEKLY WORLD NEWS
Bat Boy Lives!
Sterling
The weird, the wacky, the ridiculous

SCHIRRIPA, STEVEN R. AND CHARLES FLEMING
Nicky Deuce: Welcome to the Family
Delacorte
Moving from the burbs to Brooklyn

SCOTT, KIERAN
I Was a Non-Blonde Cheerleader
Putnam's
Rejecting the peroxide means being a reject

SEVENTEEN MAGAZINE, EDITORS
Traumarama!
Hearst
Most. Embarrassing. Moments. Ever.

SHELDON, DYAN
Sophie Pitt-Turnbull Discovers America
Candlewick
Lost luggage, no A/C, horrors on the subway

YOO, DAVID
Girls For Breakfast
Delacorte
Longing to leave social Siberia

Science Fiction

ADLINGTON, L.J.
The Diary of Pelly D
Greenwillow
Reveals the war Toni V thought he understood

BLACKMAN, MALORIE
Naughts & Crosses
Simon & Schuster
Love in a world where black rules white

BUTLER, OCTAVIA E.
Fledgling
Seven Stories
Shori, a vampire, living in daylight hours

CRAIG, JOE
Jimmy Coates: Assassin?
HarperCollins
Schoolboy and secret weapon

GOOBIE, BETH
Flux
Orca
Chased by a gang into another dimension

JEAPES, BEN
The New World Order
David Fickling
When aliens invade Cromwell's England

LEVITIN, SONIA
The Goodness Gene
Dutton
Fighting destiny to overcome evil

MCNAUGHTON, JANET
The Secret Under My Skin
EOS
Uncovering Blay's past, saving Earth's future

PATTERSON, JAMES
Maximum Ride: The Angel Experiment
Little, Brown
A winged teen protecting her family

PRATCHETT, TERRY
Only You Can Save Mankind
HarperCollins
Video game aliens surrender

SLEATOR, WILLIAM
The Last Universe
Amulet
Susan, healing her brother, risking her world

STAHLER, DAVID, JR.
Truesight
EOS
Cursed with sight in a blind world

VALENTINE, JAMES
Jump-Man
Simon & Schuster
Time-traveling Theo wrecks Jules' romance

WERLIN, NANCY
Double Helix
Dial
Eli uncovering his own genetic secrets

WESTERFELD, SCOTT
*Pretties
Simon Pulse
Keep her new life or her promise

WESTERFELD, SCOTT
*Uglies
Simon Pulse
Discovering the true cost of being pretty

Fantasy

AVI
*The Book Without Words
Hyperion
Revealing secrets of medieval magic

BENNETT, HOLLY
*The Bonemender
Orca
Using her healing powers, falling in love

BLACK, HOLLY
*Valiant
Simon & Schuster
Faeries murdered in NYC subways

CALHOUN, DIA
*The Phoenix Dance
Farrar, Straus and Giroux
Trying to understand magic and herself

CASH, STEVE
*The MEQ
Ballantine
An ancient race that does not grow old

CHAN, GILLIAN
*The Turning
Kids Can
Helping a Green Man defeat fairies

DEARY, TERRY
*The Fire Thief
Kingfisher
Ancient Greek gods in a Victorian world

DICKINSON, JOHN
*The Widow and the King
David Fickling
Growing up amidst war and magic

DIVAKARUNI, CHITRA BANERJEE
*The Mirror of Fire and Dreaming
Roaring Brook
Back to old Bengal to battle evil

FUNKE, CORNELIA
*Inkspell
Chicken House
Caught inside the pages of a book

GAIMAN, NEIL
*Anansi Boys
Morrow
Children of the spider-god

GARDNER, SALLY
*I, Coriander
Dial
A fairy's daughter in 17thC London

GRUBER, MICHAEL
*The Witch's Boy
HarperTempest
Raised by a cat, a bear and a demon

HALE, SHANNON
*Princess Academy
Bloomsbury
Unexpected talents revealed

HART, J.V.
*Capt. Hook
Laura Geringer
At school, making friends and enemies

HEMINGWAY, AMANDA
*The Greeenstone Grail
Ballantine
Exploring what dreams portray

LANDON, DENA
*Shapeshifter's Quest
Dutton
Leaving her forest home to save her people

MARTIN, RAFE
*Birdwing
Arthur A, Levine
A prince: part swan, an outsider

MEYER, KAI
*The Water Mirror
Margaret K. McElderry
Teens in Venice under siege

NIX, GARTH
*Across the Wall
HarperCollins
Stories of magical worlds

PAOLINI, CHRISTOPHER
*Eldest
Knopf
More adventures of Eragon and his dragon

PARK, PAUL
*A Princess of Roumania
Tor
Her country's last hope for peace

PAVER, MICHELLE
*Wolf Brother
HarperCollins
On a dangerous journey, 6,000 years ago

PIERCE, TAMORA AND JOSEPHA SHERMAN, EDITORS
*Young Warriors
Random House
Stories of destinies fulfilled

PRATCHETT, TERRY
*Thud!
HarperCollins
Keeping the peace among dwarves and trolls

RIORDAN, RICK
*The Lightning Thief
Miramax
Gods and monsters in Percy's world

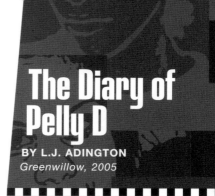

The Diary of Pelly D

BY L.J. ADINGTON
Greenwillow, 2005

A few more of the older kids are missing from school, I'm sure of it. Does no one else notice these things? It's probably something to do with the lists on the Big Screens in the main hall. A lot of students pretend to be excited to get the summons to City One—the Big One.

It's all bright lights there & loud music. City Five's so-o-o-o-o rustic, they say.

Yeah, we're rustic. We've got grass as green as the stamps on all our hands. You don't have to be a political genius to see what's going on here. The CCTV cameras have quadrupled in the last couple of weeks. Who's watching all the screens?

Poison

BY CHRIS WOODING
Orchard Books, 2005

Poison knew all about the Many-Sided War — or at least she knew the legends, for who knew what was fact and what was fiction? — but she liked to hear the old man talk. Fleet was regarded as an oddity, much as she was. Though he kept to himself, he was absent for long periods at a time, and when he returned it was always with new tales to tell. He might have been inoffensive in other ways, but the fact that he wandered at all was enough for parents to warn their children away from him. No good could come of the outside world. Phaeries lived out there, and trolls and ghoblins and things without names. There were not a few in the village who muttered that maybe the old man had a bit of phaerie in him. To be so spry at his age could only mean trouble.

On Stage

SIMMONS, DANNY, EDITOR
Russell Simmons Def Poetry Jam on Broadway & More
Atria
The energy and impact of the spoken word

TEACHOUT, TERRY
All in the Dances
Harcourt
Balanchine, master choreographer

Art: Vision Becomes Image

CHALMERS, CATHERINE
Food Chain
Aperture
Eat or be eaten

COCKCROFT, JAMES D., ASSISTED BY JANE CANNING
Latino Visions
Watts
Contemporary artists of the Americas

GANZ, NICHOLAS
*Graffiti World
Abrams
Street art from five continents

GOULART, RON
Comic Book Culture
Collectors
Everyone's old favorites

GREENBERG, JAN
Vincent van Gogh
Delacorte
The mad Dutch genius

GREENBERG, JAN AND SANDRA JORDAN
Andy Warhol
Delacorte
Fabulous Prince of Pop
Runaway Girl
Abrams
The artist Louise Bourgeois

HARING, KEITH
Dogs
Bulfinch
Words and drawings of the bold artist

HIGHSMITH, CAROL M. AND TED LANDPHAIR
America's Engineering Marvels
Gramercy
Masterworks to inspire

HILL, LABAN CARRICK
*Casa Azul
Watson-Guptill
Going back in time to meet Frida Kahlo

HOYE, JACOB
Boards
Universe
The art and design of the skateboard

KASSINGER, RUTH G.
Ceramics
Twenty-First Century
From magic pots to man-made bones

MURRAY, ELIZABETH
*Popped Art
The Museum of Modern Art
When paintings jump off the wall

RADEVSKY, ANTON
*Architecture
Universe
Classic buildings from all eras pop up

REES, ELIZABETH M.
*The Wedding
Watson-Guptill
Seeing within a Van Eyck painting

ROBBINS, TRINA
From Girls to Grrrlz
Chronicle
Nearly 60 years of women in comics

RUBIN, SUSAN GOLDMAN
Margaret Bourke-White
Abrams
Her life, her photos

SANDLER, MARTIN W.
*America Through the Lens
Henry Holt
Photographers who changed the nation

SCHIAFFINO, MARIAROSA
Goya
Peter Bedrick
Painting royal portraits and the political scene

SCHULKE, FLIP
Witness to Our Times
Cricket
Life as a photojournalist

SUTHERLAND, PETER
Autograf
powerHouse
Photos of NYC graffiti writers

TATHAM, CAROLINE AND JULIAN SEAMAN
Fashion
Barron's
A guide for the aspiring designer

Graphic Novels and Manga

CLUGSTON, CHYNNA
*Queen Bee
Scholastic
Mean girls with ESP

IKEZAWA, SATOMI
*Guru Guru Pon-Chan
Del Rey
From cute puppy to a cuter girl

JOHNSON, R. KIKUO
*Night Fisher
Fantagraphics
Even in Hawaii high school isn't a paradise

KNEECE, MARK AND JULIE COLLINS-ROSSEAU
*Trailers
NBM
Josh, covering up a killing for his mom

MATOH, SANAMI
*By the Sword
ADV Manga
Demon hunter seeking the perfect weapon

MELTZER, BRAD, RAGS MORALES AND MICHAEL BAIR
*Identity Crisis
DC Comics
Every superheroes' choice to make

MORRISON, GRANT AND FRANK QUITELY
*WE3
Vertigo
From cuddly pets to lethal weapons

NINOMIYA, TOMOKO
*Nodame Cantabile
De Rey
Piano lessons from a quirky classmate

NONAKA, EIJI
*Cromartie High School, Vol. 1
ADVManga
A gorilla, a robot and the city's bad boys

OHBA, TSUGUMI
*Death Note
VIZ Media
Killing evildoers to create a better world

SMITH, JEFF
*Out From Boneville
Graphix
Meet the Bones in a full-color world

YAZAWA, AI
*Nana
VIZ Media
Two girls, same name, new lives in Tokyo

Young Love

BRADLEY, ALEX
*24 Girls in 7 Days
Dutton
Online dating ad: big fun or big disaster

EARLS, NICK
*After Summer
Graphia
A fling on the Australian coast

FARLEY, TERRI
*Seven Tears into the Sea
Simon Pulse
To the shore, reclaiming her destiny

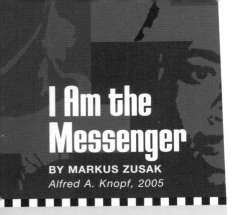

I Am the Messenger

BY MARKUS ZUSAK
Alfred A. Knopf, 2005

I'm reading the Ace of Clubs, expecting another list of addresses.

I'm wrong.

Typically, it's not going to be that easy There are no addresses this time. There's no uniform to this. There's nothing to make any part of it secure. Each part is a test, and part of that is in the unexpected.

This time, it's words.

Only words.

The card reads:

say a prayer

at the stones of home

FLAKE, SHARON G.
Who Am I Without Him?
Jump at the Sun/Hyperion
Girls and the boys in their lives

JOHNSON, ANGELA
The First Part Last
Simon & Schuster
Turning 16, becoming a father

KANTOR, MELISSA
If I Have a Wicked Stepmother, Where's My Prince?
Hyperion
Prince Charming: sport stud or art geek?

KROVATIN, CHRISTOPHER
Heavy Metal and You
Push
Metalhead goes straight-edge for love

LEVITHAN, DAVID
The Realm of Possibility
Knopf
The endless ways kids connect

MANNING, SARRA
Pretty Things
Dutton
Brie loves Charlie loves Walker loves Daisy

RUSHTON, ROSIE
The Dashwood Sisters' Secret of Love
Hyperion
3 beauties + 3 beaus = 1 hot pursuit

VAIL, RACHEL
If We Kiss
HarperCollins
Fixated on a bad boy's lips

WHITCOMB, LAURA
A Certain Slant of Light
Graphia
When ghost falls for ghost

WILLIAMS-GARCIA, RITA
Every Time a Rainbow Dies
HarperCollins
A victim of rape changes Thulani's life

WOODSON, JACQUELINE
Behind You
Putnam's
Moving on after losing a loved one

Mystery and Suspense

ALPHIN, ELAINE MARIE
The Perfect Shot
Carolrhoda
Brian, inspired to uncover the truth

BARRETT, TRACY
Cold in Summer
Henry Holt
New town, new friends, old ghosts

COLLIER, JAMES LINCOLN
The Empty Mirror
Bloomsbury
When two souls claim one body

CONNOR, LESLIE
Dead on Town Line
Dial
Cassie: "It's me they're searching for"

COONEY, CAROLINE B.
Code Orange
Delacorte
A biology paper hazardous to NYC's health

CORMIER, ROBERT
The Rag and Bone Shop
Delacorte
Murder-true or false confession?

DEUKER, CARL
Runner
Houghton Mifflin
Chance, paying the price for a dangerous job

GILES, GAIL
Playing in Traffic
Roaring Brook
Shy Matt and the wild goth-girl

GROSS, PHILIP
Turn to Stone
Dial
Living statues may not stay that way

HADDIX, MARGARET PETERSON
Escape From Memory
Simon & Schuster
Family secrets hidden in Kira's brain

KEHRET, PEG
The Ghost's Grave
Dutton
Josh: helping a ghost, finding a cashbox

LIPPMAN, LAURA
To the Power of Three
Morrow
A friendship destroyed by a school shooting

MADISON, BENNETT
Lulu Dark Can See Through Walls
Razorbill
A stolen purse, a missing girl, a murder

MCALPINE, GORDON
Mystery Box
Cricket
Falling in love and solving crimes

MCNAMEE, GRAHAM
Acceleration
Wendy Lamb
Duncan stalking a serial killer

MORGENROTH, KATE
Jude
Simon & Schuster
Surviving an unfair, stiff sentence

PLUM-UCCI, CAROL
The She
Harcourt
Disappearing parents swallowed by the sea

PRIESTLEY, CHRIS
Death and the Arrow
Knopf
Gruesome serial killings in 1715

SCRIMGER, RICHARD
From Charlie's Point of View
Dutton
Proving his father isn't the ATM bandit

SIMMONS, MICHAEL
Finding Lubchenko
Razorbill
Evan pursuing a murderer to free his father

WATSON, JUDE
Premonitions
Scholastic
Gracie, using ESP to save her friend

WEATHERLY, LEE
Missing Abby
David Fickling
When a 13-year old girl vanished

WYNNE-JONES, TIM
***A Thief in the House of Memory**
Farrar, Straus and Giroux
Declan: suspecting his own father

ZUSAK, MARKUS
***I Am the Messenger**
Knopf
Ed: on a mission guided by playing cards

Horror

ALLIE, SCOTT, EDITOR
The Dark Horse Book of Witchcraft
Dark Horse
Powerful women, supernatural skill

BLOOR, EDWARD
Story Time
Harcourt
Where testing is the work of the devil

DUNKLE, CLARE B.
***By These Ten Bones**
Henry Holt
An ancient evil in Medieval Scotland

HOROWITZ, ANTHONY
***Raven's Gate**
Scholastic
A creepy place where death abounds

HURSTON, ZORA NEALE, COLLECTOR; ADAPTED BY JOYCE CAROL THOMAS
The Skull Talks Back and Other Haunting Tales
HarperCollins
Spooky tales from folklore

MCKINLEY, ROBIN
Sunshine
Berkley
Saving herself from being a vampire meal

METZ, MELINDA
Raven's Point
HarperCollins
Ancient evil on a small island

MEYER, STEPHENIE
***Twilight**
Little, Brown
When your hot new boyfriend drinks blood

NOYES, DEBORAH, EDITOR
Gothic!
Candlewick
Ten original dark tales

RICE, ANNE
Interview with the Vampire
Ballantine
Vampire tells all to reporter

RICHARDSON, E.E.
***Devil's Footsteps**
Delacorte
A dark force stalking the town's children

SAUL, JOHN
Black Creek Crossing
Ballantine
Life in a charming, haunted house

SHAN, DARREN
***Lord Loss**
Little, Brown
A family murdered by demons

SHUSTERMAN, NEAL
***Dread Locks**
Dutton
A beautiful girl with terrible powers

SLEATOR, WILLIAM
The Boy Who Couldn't Die
Amulet
The boy who could kill

SOSNOWSKI, DAVID
Vamped
Free Press
When there are more vampires than humans

WATTS, LEANDER
***Ten Thousand Charms**
Houghton Mifflin
Blackmail, murder and evil spirits

WESTERFELD, SCOTT
***Peeps**
Razorbill
When sex turns deadly

WOODING, CHRIS
The Haunting of Alaizabel Cray
Orchard
Terror in the London streets

Poetry

ACHEBE, CHINUA
Collected Poems
Anchor
Nigeria's powerful writer

ALVAREZ, JULIA
The Woman I Kept to Myself
Algonquin
Wise and personal words

COLLINS, BILLY
***The Trouble With Poetry**
Random House
The unique voice of NY's Poet Laureate

COLLINS, BILLY, EDITOR
***180 More**
Random House
Accessible, contemporary, extraordinary

ESPADA, MARTÍN
Alabanza
Norton
A Latino lyric voice

JANECZKO, PAUL B., EDITOR
Blushing
Orchard
Expressions of love

JORDAN, A. VAN
M-A-C-N-O-L-I-A
Norton
Story of a spelling whiz

JUSTICE, DONALD
Collected Poems
Knopf
The master of simple, classical form

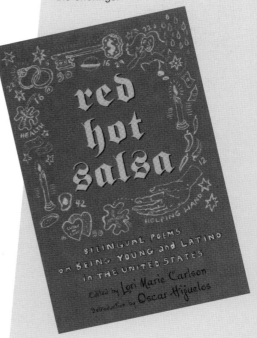

Red Hot Salsa

BY LORI MARIE CARLSON, EDITOR
Henry Holt and Company, 2005

One of the obvious outcomes of the Latin American immigration to this land is the acknowledgment by our society and the media of the amazing contributions of Latinos of all walks of life and ethnicities to the dynamism of the nation. In the fields of science, arts and letters, military service, public affairs, entertainment, fashion, and food, Latin Americans and Latinos of several generations are offering our country their best. And they are helping to transform the notion of what it means to be a proud American.

The contributions of Latino writers to the American canon continue to grow. This is particularly true of Latino poets. There is so much exceptional poetry being published today—so much that in my meanderings through libraries, schools, cultural institutions, bookstores, and churches, I found myself dizzied by the offerings.

KEILLOR, GARRISON, EDITOR
Good Poems For Hard Times
Viking
Words that give courage

MOSS, THYLIAS
Slave Moth
Persea
An enslaved girl imagining freedom

MYERS, WALTER DEAN
Here in Harlem
Holiday House
Honoring his hometown

PARISI, JOSEPH, EDITOR
100 Essential Modern Poems
Ivan R. Dee
Expressing feelings we all feel

PARKS, GORDON
Eyes With Winged Thoughts
Atria
Words and photos from an American master

PAWLAK, MARK AND DICK LOURIE, EDITORS WITH RON SCHREIBER AND ROBERT
Shooting the Rat
Hanging Loose
Stories and poems by high school writers

PERDOMO, WILLIE
Smoking Lovely
Rattapallax
Our Nuyorican laureate

PINSKY, ROBERT AND MAGGIE DIETZ, EDITORS
An Invitation to Poetry
Norton
From the Favorite Poem Project

ROSENBERG, LIZ AND DEENA NOVEMBER
I Just Hope It's Lethal
Graphia
Struggles with life's worst moments

SCHMIDT, ELIZABETH AND KEVIN YOUNG
Poems of New York
Random House
The icons of our city

SCHULTZ, PHILIP
Living in the Past
Harcourt
Rochester, New York, in the fifties

SESHADRI, VIJAY
The Long Meadow
Graywolf
From India to Brooklyn

SHANGE, NTOZAKE, FRANK STEWART, AND KAMOINGE INC.
The Sweet Breath of Life
Atria
Words, images: the African-American family

SNYDER, JANE MCINTOSH AND CAMILLE-YVETTE WELSCH
Sappho
Chelsea House
Her words of love from 2600 years ago

TENNYSON, ALFRED, LORD WITH ILLUSTRATIONS BY GENEVIÉVE CÔTÉ
The Lady of Shalott
Kids Can
A haunting portrait of unrequited love

VECCHIONE, PATRICE, EDITOR
Revenge and Forgiveness
Henry Holt
Timeless human desires

WRITERSCORPS
Paint Me Like I Am
HarperTempest
Lively teen voices

YOUNG, KEVIN
To Repel Ghosts
Knopf
Jean-Michel Basquiat: the artist in verse

The Movies and TV

ALEXANDER, GEORGE
Why We Make Movies
Broadway
Black filmmakers talking

BIZONY, PIERS
Digital Domain
Billboard
Creating special effects

DUNCAN, JODY
Star Wars: Mythmaking
Del Rey
Behind the scenes with color photos

FRIEDMAN, DIANA
Sitcom Style
Clarkson Potter
Inside America's favorite TV homes

HACKFORD, TAYLOR, JAMES L. WHITE AND LINDA SUNSHINE
Ray
Newmarket
A tribute to Ray Charles

LUMME, HELENA
Great Women of Film
Billboard
Actresses, producers, directors, and more

RICHMOND, RAY
This is Jeopardy!
Barnes & Noble
Celebrating America's favorite quiz show

ROEPER, RICHARD
10 Sure Signs a Movie Character is Doomed, and Other Surprising Movie Lists
Hyperion
The best, the worst and more

RUBIN, SUSAN GOLDMAN
Steven Spielberg
Abrams
Crazy for movies since he was a child

VAZ, MARK COTTA
The Art of Star Wars
Del Rey
Episode II: Attack of the clones.

WORMSER, RICHARD
To the Young Filmmaker
Watts
Conversations with working filmmakers

Teen Novels and Short Stories

ADOFF, JAIME
Jimi & Me
Jump at the Sun
Keith, penniless after his father's murder

AMATEAU, GIGI
Claiming Georgia Tate
Candlewick
Away from her father's abusive hands

ANDERSON, LAURIE HALSE
Prom
Viking
Senior gala saved by the underdog

BANERJEE, ANJALI
Maya Running
Wendy Lamb
Brown skin girl trapped in a blue jean world

BAPTISTE, TRACEY
Angel's Grace
Simon & Schuster
NYC girl tracking her father in Trinidad

BAUER, JOAN
Best Foot Forward
Putnam's
Love and life found among the shoelaces

BRIAN, KATE
Lucky T
Simon & Schuster
Carrie's life wrecked by a lost t-shirt

BROOKS, KEVIN
Candy
Chicken House
Love: sweeter than addiction

CABOT, MEG
Ready or Not
HarperCollins
The ups and downs of dating The First Son

Looking for Alaska

BY JOHN GREEN
Dutton Books, 2005

We walked five doors down to Room 48. A dry-erase board was taped to the door using duct tape. In blue marker, it read: *Alaska has a single!*

The Colonel explained to me that 1. this was Alaska's room, and that 2. she had a single room because the girl who was supposed to be her roommate got kicked out at the end of last year, and that 3. Alaska had cigarettes, although the Colonel neglected to ask whether 4. I smoked, which 5. I didn't.

He knocked once, loudly. Through the door, a voice screamed, "Oh my God come in you short little man because I have the best story."

We walked in. I turned to close the door behind me, and the Colonel shook his head and said, "After seven, you have to leave the door open if you're in a girl's room," but I barely heard him because the hottest girl in all of human history was standing before me in cutoff jeans and a peach tank top. And she was talking over the Colonel, talking loud and fast.

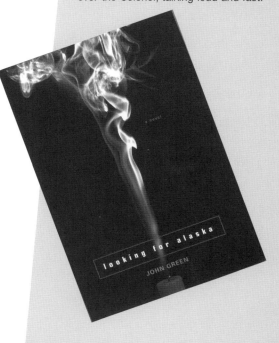

Inexcusable

BY CHRIS LYNCH
*Gennie Seo
Books/Atheneum, 2005*

Good guys don't do bad things. Good guys understand that no means no, and so I could not have done this because I understand, and I love Gigi Boudakian.

"I love you, Gigi."

As I say this, Gigi Boudakian lets out the most horrific scream I have ever heard, and I am terrified by it and reach out, lunge toward her and try and cover her mouth with my hands and I fall over her and she screams louder and bites at my hands and I keep flailing, trying to stop that sound coming out of her and getting out into the world.

I am only trying to stop the sound. It looks terrible what I am doing, as I watch my hands doing it, as I watch hysterical Gigi Boudakian reacting to me, and it looks really, really terrible but I am only trying to stop the awful sound and the way it looks is not the way it is.

The way it looks is *not* the way it is.

chris lynch

a novel

LION, MELISSA
Upstream
Wendy Lamb
Moving on after a boyfriend's freak death

LOCKHART, E.
The Boyfriend List
Delacorte
From popular to putrid in ten days

LUBAR, DAVID
Sleeping Freshmen Never Lie
Dutton
Humorous, humiliating, horrible high school

LYNCH, CHRIS
Inexcusable
Atheneum
Son, brother, liar, rapist
Me, Dead Dad, & Alcatraz
HarperCollins
Elvin's uncle, back from the dead

MACKLER, CAROLYN
Vegan Virgin Valentine
Candlewick
Control freak ready to break out

MALKIN, NINA
6X: The Uncensored Confessions
Scholastic
Bombshell, Bumpkin, Boss Lady + Boy = 1 Band

MCCORMICK, PATRICIA
My Brother's Keeper
Hyperion
Jake: seriously on the verge of burnout

MCGHEE, ALISON
All Rivers Flow to the Sea
Candlewick
Paralyzed by her sister's coma

MERCADO, NANCY E., EDITOR
*** Every Man For Himself***
Dial
10 stories: geeks, princes, BB guns, bar mitzvahs

MOORE, PETER
Caught in the Act
Viking
Ethan intoxicated by love and danger

MYERS, WALTER DEAN WITH ART BY CHRISTOPHER MYERS
Autobiography of My Dead Brother
HarperTempest
When a best friend deals drugs

MYRACLE, LAUREN
Rhymes with Witches
Amulet
Paying for popularity with a wicked price

NELSON, R.A.
Teach Me
Razorbill
Student & teacher: poetry, love, obsession

NEWMAN, LESLÉA
Jailbait
Delacorte
Andi falling for 40-year old Frank

NILSSON, PER
You & You & You
Front Street
Three lives: three unexpected turns

NOËL, ALYSON
Art Geeks and Prom Queens
St. Martin's Griffin
Clawing her way to the top of the A-list

PAPADEMETRIOU, LISA AND CHRIS TEBBETTS
M or F?
Razorbill
Falling for the unknown in a chat room

PEARSON, MARY E.
A Room on Lorelei Street
Henry Holt
Freedom found in the guise of a lit window

PERKINS, LYNNE RAE
Criss Cross
Greenwillow
Five friends intersect, connect, discover

QUALEY, MARSHA
Just Like That
Dial
Hanna, breaking it off and moving on

RAPP, ADAM
Under the Wolf, Under the Dog
Candlewick
Struggling to cope with a violent past

ROBERTS, LAURA PEYTON
The Queen of Second Place
Delacorte
Vying for first place in romance

ROSOFF, MEG
How I Live Now
Wendy Lamb
The bonds that form in a time of war

ROTH, MATTHUE
Never Mind the Goldbergs
Push
Hava, the Hasidic Hollywood heroine

SINGER, MARILYN, EDITOR
Make Me Over
Dutton
Reinvention stories: more than a makeover

SITOMER, ALAN LAWRENCE
The Hoopster
Jump at the Sun
Andre, from the court to the printed page

SONES, SONYA
One of Those Hideous Books Where the Mother Dies
Simon & Schuster
Starting over in LA with a movie-star dad

SONNENBLICK, JORDAN
Drums, Girls & Dangerous Pie
Scholastic
Steve's life and brother ravaged by cancer

STEPHENSON, LYNDA
Dancing With Elvis
Eerdmans
Frankilee: bright, sassy, ready for change

VEGA, DENISE
*Click Here
Little, Brown
Private blog goes public: disaster

VIZZINI, NED
Be More Chill
Hyperion
Transformed by a pill from dork to hottie

VOLPONI, PAUL
*Black and White
Viking
Taking the rap for your best friend's crime

WEAVER, WILL
*Full Service
Farrar, Straus and Giroux
Paul: getting a job and a life

WITTLINGER, ELLEN
*Sandpiper
Simon & Schuster
When rejection turns to revenge

WONG, JOYCE LEE
*Seeing Emily
Amulet
Off to Taipei, discovering her heritage

Novels and Short Stories

ATWOOD, MARGARET
*The Penelopiad
Canongate
Retelling the myth of Odysseus' wife

BATES, JUDY FONG
*Midnight at the Dragon Cafe
Counterpoint
Annie's fateful summer of secrets

BEARD, PHILIP
*Dear Zoe
Viking
Coming to terms with a sister's death

BERLIN, ADAM
Belmondo Style
St. Martin's
On the run from the NYC police

BOYLE, T.C.
*The Human Fly and Other Stories
Viking
Imaginative glimpses of teen protagonists

BUCKHANON, KALISHA
*Upstate
St. Martin's
Love stands the test of time and prison

CALDWELL, IAN AND DUSTIN THOMASON
The Rule of Four
Dial
Two Princeton seniors' amazing discovery

CURRAN, COLLEEN
*Whores on the Hill
Vintage
Three friends, taking on the world

DANTICAT, EDWIDGE
The Dew Breaker
Knopf
The torturer's daughter, unraveling secrets

DAWESAR, ABHA
*Babyji
Anchor
Pushing sexual boundaries in India

DE HAVEN, TOM
*It's Superman!
Chronicle
Clark, discovering his powers

DERMANSKY, MARCY
*Twins
Morrow
Blond, beautiful and tormented

ERIAN, ALICIA
*Towelhead
Simon & Schuster
Facing the dangers of sexual awakening

EVANS, DIANA
*26a
Morrow
Biracial twins finding their identity

FELDMAN, ELLEN
*The Boy Who Loved Anne Frank
Norton
Peter in America, reliving the past

FISHCHER, JACKIE MOYER
An Egg on Three Sticks
Thomas Dunne
First love shadowed by mental illness

FLOCK, ELIZABETH
*Me & Emma
Mira
Sisters enduring a poor, violent home

FOER, JONATHAN SAFRAN
*Extremely Loud and Incredibly Close
Houghton Mifflin
A brilliant boy's search for truth in NYC

GABHART, ANN H.
*The Scent of Lilacs
Revell
Jocie's discoveries about family secrets

HADDON, MARK
The Curious Incident of the Dog in the Night-Time
Doubleday
An autistic boy playing Sherlock

HALPIN, BRENDAN
Donorboy
Random House
Sudden fatherhood for a sperm donor

HOFFMAN, ALICE
Blackbird House
Doubleday
200 years of love and loss

HYLAND, M. J.
How the Light Gets In
Canongate
An unhappy exchange student in Chicago

LANDVIK, LORNA
*Oh My Stars
Ballantine
Starting over, managing a band

It's Superman!
BY TOM DE HAVEN
Chronicle Books, 2005

At school Clark is not actively disliked, he isn't *un*popular, he's just... there. There-but-not-there. You say hello, he says hello back. You don't, he doesn't. Overall, he's good-enough *looking,* but not what you would call handsome, either. His ears are too small for his head, and his crowded teeth crooked on the bottom. He's a quiet boy, a struggling B student, does all of his homework, and while it seems by appearances that he'd be strong, well-coordinated, quick—he has good shoulders and graceful legs—he has never gone out for athletics. And he was invited to by coaches any number of times. He reads a lot, but mostly the junkiest, dopiest pulps, the kind with tentacled green Martians on the covers. He likes movies, all sorts of movies, and often goes by himself. Even still goes to the kiddie show on Saturday mornings because he especially likes chapter-plays with cowboys and masked men, death rays and robots. And he writes—carefully, accurately, but with no special flair—for the school newspaper. He's okay. He's all right. In the opinion of his peers at Smallville High School, Clark is all right but nothing special.

LEE, MARIE MYUNG-OK
Somebody's Daughter
Beacon
Exploring her Korean heritage

LLOYD, DAVID
Boys
Syracuse Univ. Rowdy, friendly, shocking, and real
Rowdy, friendly, shocking and real

LYNCH, JIM
The Highest Tide
Bloomsbury
Where mysteries of life might be found

MAILLARD, KEITH
Running
Brindle & Glass
John, on the rocky road toward adulthood

MARSHALL, BEV
Hot Fudge Sundae Blues
Ballantine
The trouble that lies can cause

MCDONELL, NICK
The Third Brother
Grove
A family tragedy in the midst of 9/11

MENO, JOE
Hairstyles of the Damned
Akashic/Punk Planet
Brian, falling for a tough punk rocker

OYEYEMI, HELEN
The Icarus Girl
Nan. A. Talese
A haunting presence discovered in Nigeria

PARKER, MICHAEL
If You Want Me to Stay
Algonquin
Holding a family together without parents

PARKS, SUZAN-LORI
Getting Mother's Body
Random House
Pregnant Billy, 16, robbing a grave

PORTER, CONNIE
Imani All Mine
Mariner
Tasha, 15, and now a mother

RAWLES, NANCY
My Jim
Crown
A love so deep lost nearly forever

SAMBROOK, CLARE
Hide & Seek
Canongate
A family's loss of a child

SAPPHIRE
Push
Vintage
Precious, an abused survivor, speaks

SHEPARD, JIM
Project X
Knopf
Two eighth-grade loners taking revenge

SHREVE, ANITA
Light on Snow
Little, Brown
Finding an abandoned baby in the woods

SIDDONS, ANNE RIVERS
Sweetwater Creek
HarperCollins
Emily's Southern world, threatened

SITTENFELD, CURTIS
Prep
Random House
Boarding school blues

SLOAN, KAY
The Patron Saint of Red Chevys
Permanent
Teen age girls looking for a mother's killer

STRAUSE, BRIAN
Maybe a Miracle
Ballantine
A family crisis, a test of faith

Rap, Rock and Bach

50 CENT
From Pieces to Weight
MTV Books
Good times and bad in Southside Queens

BALTIN, STEVE
From the Inside
Bradson
Linkin Park's *Meteora* tour

BOZZA, ANTHONY
Whatever You Say I Am
Crown
The life and times of Eminem

CHANG, JEFF
Can't Stop Won't Stop
St. Martin's
History of the hip-hop generation

CHIRAZI, STEFFAN, EDITOR
So What!
Broadway
Metallica, the official chronicle

CROSS, CHARLES R.
Room Full of Mirrors
Hyperion
Guitar god, Jimi Hendrix

GETZINGER, DONNA AND DANIEL FELSENFELD
Johann Sebastian Bach
Morgan Reynolds
A life in music

GOBI
Thru My Eyes
Atria
A friend's view of Tupac's last year

GUERASEVA, STACY
Def Jam, Inc.
One World
World's most influential hip-hop label

HERMES, WILL, EDITOR WITH SIA MICHEL
SPIN: 20 Years of Alternative Music
Three Rivers
Rock, hip-hop, techno and beyond

HOYE, JACOB AND KAROLYN ALI, EDITORS
Tupac: Resurrection 1971-1996
Atria
Still life in words and pictures

KRISTAL, HILLY AND TAMAR BRAZIS, EDITOR
CBGB & OMFUG
Abrams
The club where NYC punk was born

MALONE, BONZ; NICOLE BATTLE AND DJ LINDY
Hip Hop Immortals
Thunder's Mouth
Photographers capturing entertainers

MARSALIS, WYNTON WITH ILLUSTRATIONS BY PAUL ROGERS
Jazz ABZ
Candlewick
Portraits in poetry from Armstrong to Dizzy

OH, MINYA
Bling Bling
Wenner
Hip-hop's love affair with jewelry

PARTRIDGE, ELIZABETH
John Lennon: All I Want is the Truth
Viking
Rebel, Beatle, legend

ROBERTS, JEREMY
Bob Dylan
Lerner
The voice of a generation

RODRIGUEZ-DUARTE, ALEXIS
Presenting Celia Cruz
Clarkson Potter
The Cuban born Queen of Salsa

SCRIMGEOUR, DIANA
U2 Show
Riverhead
Twenty-five years on tour

TANNER, MIKE
Resurrection Blues
Annick
Flynn's rock 'n' roll life at 15

WASFIE, GISELLE ZADO
*So Fly
St. Martin's Griffin
Sophie in the NYC hip-hop scene

WHITELAW, PAUL
*Belle and Sebastian
St. Martin's Griffin
The rise of an indie-rock band

Historical Fiction

ALLENDE, ISABEL
*Zorro
HarperCollins
How the legend began

ANDERSON, LAURIE HALSE
Fever 1793
Simon & Schuster
Enduring the deadly epidemic

BANKS, LYNNE REID
*Tiger, Tiger
Delacorte
Brother cubs escaping Ancient Rome

CARBONE, ELISA
*Last Dance on Holladay Street
Knopf
Finding her mother and her identity in the frontier west

CEELY, JONATHA
*Bread and Dreams
Delacorte
Mina, 1848, baking her way to the Erie Canal

CROWE, CHRIS
Mississippi Trial
Phyllis Fogelman
The summer Emmett Till was murdered

DONNELLY, JENNIFER
A Northern Light
Harcourt
A girl's dreams disturbed by murder

GRANT, K.M.
*Blood Red Horse
Walker
Gavin and William off to the Crusades

HASSINGER, PETER W.
Shakespeare's Daughter
Laura Geringer
Who wanted to be a singer

HESSE, KAREN
Witness
Scholastic
When the Ku Klux Klan comes to Vermont

HOFFMAN, ALICE
*The Foretelling
Little, Brown
Rain, destined to be queen in a time without men

INGOLD, JEANETTE
*Hitch
Harcourt
Moss, jobless and homeless during the Great Depression

LAWLOR, LAURIE
*Dead Reckoning
Simon and Schuster
Emmet sailing the seas with Captain Francis Drake

LAWRENCE, IAIN
B for Buster
Delacorte
16 and flying bombing raids over Germany

LERANGIS, PETER
*Smiler's Bones
Scholastic
When Inuit people were museum objects

LESTER, JULIUS
*Day of Tears
Jump at the Sun
Voices from the largest slave auction in America

LEVINE, ELLEN
*Catch a Tiger by the Toe
Viking
A family under siege during the 1950's "Red scare"

MCCAUGHREAN, GERALDINE
*Not the End of the World
HarperTempest
Timna, forty days and forty nights on the Ark

MCKERNAN, VICTORIA
*Shackleton's Stowaway
Knopf
Surviving a shipwreck in the frozen Antarctic

MEYER, CAROLYN
*Marie, Dancing
Harcourt
"The Little Dancer" posing for the artist Edgar Degas

MOLLOY, MICHAEL
*Peter Raven Under Fire
Chicken House
Pirates and the Napoleonic wars

REES, CELIA
Pirates!
Bloomsbury
Girls seeking treasure

UPDALE, ELEANOR
Montmorency: Thief, Liar, Gentleman?
Orchard
Master and servant in one body

WILSON, DIANE LEE
*Black Storm Comin'
Margaret McElderry
Colton riding the Pony Express for family and freedom

*new book title

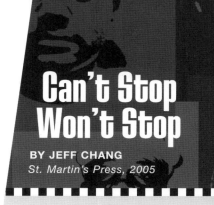

Can't Stop Won't Stop

BY JEFF CHANG
St. Martin's Press, 2005

My own feeling is that the idea of the Hip-Hop Generation brings together time and race, place and polyculturalism, hot beats and hybridity. It describes the turn from politics to culture, the process of entropy and reconstruction. It captures the collective hopes and nightmares, ambitions and failures of those who would otherwise be described as "post-this" or "post-that."

So, you ask, when does the Hip-Hop Generation begin? After DJ Kool Herc and Afrika Bambaataa. Whom does it include? Anyone who is down. When does it end? When the next generation tells us it's over.

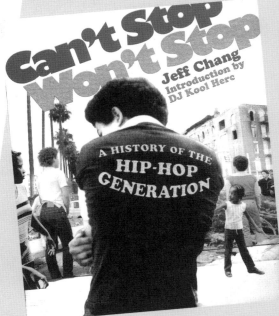

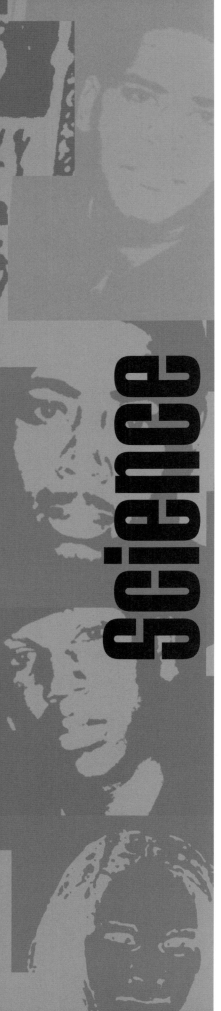

science

Brain Food

BARNARD, BRYN
*Outbreak
Crown
How microbes shape civilization

BRYSON, BILL
A Short History of Nearly Everything
Broadway
And how we know what we know

CARLSON, DALE
In and Out of Your Mind
Bick
How science applies to your life

CURTIS, BRYAN, EDITOR
The Explainer
Anchor
Questions we never think to ask

DENDY, LESLIE AND MEL BORING
*Guinea Pig Scientists
Henry Holt
Risking their own lives to save the lives of others

FALK, DAN
Universe on a T-Shirt
Arcade
Searching for the Holy Grail

FELDMAN, DAVID
Do Elephants Jump?
HarperCollins
Do skunks think skunks stink and more

GEE, HENRY
The Science of Middle-Earth
Cold Spring
Knowledge that enriches a fantasy classic

GRIBBIN, MARY AND JOHN GRIBBIN
*The Science of Philip Pullman's His Dark Materials
Knopf
How does the Golden Compass work?

HAWKING, STEPHEN WITH LEONARD MLODINOW
*A Briefer History of Time
Bantam
Explaining the nature of space and time

JORDAN, MICHAEL
Hush Hush
Firefly
Notorious cases of scientific secrecy

KAKALIOS, JAMES
*The Physics of Superheroes
Gotham
The science hidden in comic books

KERROD, ROBIN AND DR. SHARON ANN HOLGATE
The Way Science Works
DK
Experiments that explain our world

LE COURTEUR, PENNY & JAY BURRESON
Napoleon's Buttons
Jeremy P. Tarcher/Putnam
How history turns on atomic structure

MASOFF, JOY
Oh, Yuck!
Workman
Why snot is hot and pus is a must

MCCLAFFERTY, CARLA KILLOUGH
The Head Bone's Connected to the Neck Bone
Farrar, Straus and Giroux
The history and mystery of x-rays

OLSON, STEVE
Count Down
Houghton Mifflin
Teens take the world's hardest math test

OUELLETTE, JENNIFER
*Black Bodies and Quantum Cats
Penguin
How physicists think about the world

PATENT, DOROTHY HINSHAW
Charles Darwin
Holiday House
One of the inventors of modern science

RATHJEN, DON
Square Wheels
Exploratorium
31 projects that make science fun

RIDLEY, MATT
Nature Via Nurture
HarperCollins
Exploring the roots of human behavior

SEGAL, NANCY L.
*Indivisible by Two
Harvard Univ.
Amazing stories of extraordinary twins

SEIPLE, SAMANTHA AND TODD SEIPLE
*Mutants, Clones, and Killer Corn
Lerner
Genetically engineered plants and animals

SILVERSTEIN, ALVIN, VIRGINIA SILVERSTEIN AND LAURA SILVERSTEIN NUNN
DNA
Twenty-First Century
Revealing the code of life

SILVERSTEIN, KEN
The Radioactive Boy Scout
Random House
Building a backyard breeder reactor

The Universe and Beyond

CHAIKIN, ANDREW
Space
Firefly
Photos from The Final Frontier

DUPAS, ALAIN
Destination Mars
Firefly
The call of the red planet

JACKSON, ELLEN
Looking for Life in the Universe
Houghton Mifflin
Scientists who look for E.T.s

KERROD, ROBIN
Hubble
Firefly
Amazing images from deep space
Universe
DK
Vast space and all that it holds

MACKENZIE, DANA
The Big Splat, or How Our Moon Came to Be
Wiley
The birth of our celestial neighbor

MILLER, RON AND WILLIAM K. HARTMANN
The Grand Tour,
3rd revised edition
Workman
A new look at the solar system

RANDLES, JENNY
Breaking the Time Barrier
Paraview Pocket
The race to build the first time machine

SOBEL, DAVA
The Planets
Viking
Origins and oddities of the sun's family

TYSON, NEIL DE GRASSE, CHARLES LIU & ROBERT IRION
One Universe
Joseph Henry
Finding a connection to the cosmos

Fur, Feathers and Scales

ATTENBOROUGH, DAVID
The Life of Mammals
Princeton Univ. Press
From the pygmy shrew to the blue whale

BEHLER, JOHN L. AND DEBORAH A. BEHLER
Frogs
Sterling
All sizes, all shapes, all colors

CARWARDINE, MARK
Shark
Firefly
Man-killer or endangered species

CHALMERS, CATHERINE
American Cockroach
Aperture
Our revulsion revisited

DIBSIE, PATRICIA
Love Heels
Yorkville
Canine companions making life easier

GREEN-ARMYTAGE, STEPHEN
Extraordinary Pigeons
Abrams
Not your typical statue sitters

HALE, RACHAEL
101 Cataclysms
Bulfinch
A celebration of our feline friends
It's a Zoo Out There
Bulfinch
101 photographs of our favorite friends

HARTNETT, SONYA
Stripes of the Sidestep Wolf
Candlewick
Protecting a Tasmanian tiger

HEARNE, BETSY
The Canine Connection
Margaret K. McElderry
Stories about that special relationship

HELFER, RALPH
Zamba
HarperCollins
Animal trainer and his pet lion

KARR, KATHLEEN
Exiled
Marshall Cavendish
A camel's life in Texas

KATZ, JON
The Dogs of Bedlam Farm
Villard
Writer turned sheepherder and his dogs

LACRAMPE, CORINE
Sleep and Rest in Animals
Firefly
Do insects sleep? Do reptiles dream?

MASSON, JEFFREY MOUSSAIEFF
Raising the Peaceable Kingdom
Ballantine
Animal enemies or friends

MILLS, STEPHEN
Tiger
Firefly
Supple, powerful, long, lean, intense

MITTELBACH, MARGARET AND MICHAEL CREWDSON
Carnivorous Nights
Villard
Seeking the Tasmanian tiger

MONTGOMERY, SY
Search for the Golden Moon Bear
Houghton Mifflin
Amazing animals in the Asian jungles

RYLANT, CYNTHIA
Boris
Harcourt
Bonding with a big gray cat

SCHAFER, KEVIN
Penguin Planet
NorthWord
Comic on land, but so graceful in the sea

SIMMONDS, MARK
Whales & Dolphins of the World
MIT
The sea's most fascinating creatures

STANTON, BILL
The Tao of Maggie
Andrews McMeel
Life lessons from a Basset hound

THAYER, HELEN
Three Among the Wolves
Sasquatch
One dog, two humans, three wolf packs

WALDBAUER, GILBERT
Insights From Insects
Prometheus
What bad bugs can teach us

Outbreak

BY BRYN BARNARD
Crown, 2005

You're born pristine and alone, but it doesn't last. With your first independent breath, your body becomes a cooperative venture with other creatures: a colony, a host. You become infected.

The creatures that invade your body are called *microbes*. Invisible to the eye, so small they have to be measured in millionths of a meter, these tiny organisms are mostly single-celled bacteria. They arrive via the air you breathe, the water you drink, the surfaces you touch, and the food you eat. They colonize your skin, your hair, your mouth, your eyes, your ears, and your intestines. By the time you're an adult, you'll be carrying around about two pounds of these creatures, mostly in your gut. In sheer numbers, they'll make up 95 percent of all the cells in your body, about ten quadrillion in all.

This is a good thing.

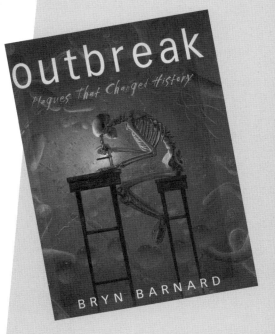

Garbage Land

BY ELIZABETH ROYTE
Little, Brown and Company, 2005

Across the nation, electronic waste is accumulating faster than anyone knows what to do with it—almost three times faster, in fact, than our overall municipal waste stream. According to the National Safety Council, nearly 250 million computers will become obsolete between 2004 and 2009. Carnegie Mellon University researchers have predicted that at least 150 million PCs will be buried in landfills by 2005, and by the following year, predicts the Silicon Valley Toxics Coalition (SVTC), some 163,420 computers and televisions will become obsolete every *day*. Where will all these gizmos go, and what impact will they have when they get there?

WALKER, SALLY M.
Fossil Fish Found Alive
Carolrhoda
Discovering the Coelacanth

WINN, MARIE
Red-Tails In Love
Pantheon
Hawks and other secrets of Central Park

ZHI, LÜ
Giant Pandas in the Wild
Aperture
Studying and saving an endangered species

Mind and Body

BRYNIE, FAITH HICKMAN
101 Questions About Food and Digestion That Have Been Eating at You... Until Now
Twenty-First Century
Why you really are what you eat

CHOROST, MICHAEL
*Rebuilt
Houghton Mifflin
A computer in his head restores one man's hearing

DAVIDSON, SUE AND BEN MORGAN
Human Body Revealed
DK
An illustrated journey through your body

FARRELL, JEANETTE
*Invisible Allies
Farrar, Straus and Giroux
They aren't germs if they insure our survival

FLEISCHMAN, JOHN
Phineas Gage
Houghton Mifflin
A gruesome advance in brain science

FRIEDLANDER, MARK P., JR.
Outbreak
Lerner
Disease detectives at work

HYMAN, BRUCE M., PH.D. AND CHERRY PEDRICH, R. N.
Obsessive-Compulsive Disorder
Twenty-First Century
Causes, symptoms and current treatment

KENT, DEBORAH
Snake Pits, Talking Cures, & Magic Bullets
Twenty-First Century
A history of mental illness

KUHN, CYNTHIA, SCOTT SWARTZWELDER AND WILKIE WILSON
Buzzed,
revised edition
Norton
The straight facts: alcohol, ecstasy, more

MURPHY, WENDY
Spare Parts
Twenty-First Century
From peg legs to gene splices

NEWQUIST, H.P.
*The Great Brain Book
Scholastic
Your most important organ

NILSSON, LENNART AND LARS HAMBERGER
A Child is Born,
4th edition
Delacorte
The miracle of human reproduction

OFRI, DANIELLE
*Incidental Findings
Beacon
Learning the art, not the science of medicine

ROACH, MARY
Stiff
Norton
The curious lives of human cadavers

SILVERSTEIN, ALVIN, VIRGINIA SILVERSTEIN AND LAURA SILVERSTEIN NUNN
Cells
Twenty-First Century
The basic units of life

SLOAN, CHRISTOPHER
Bury the Dead
National Geographic
What the customs of death reveal about us

TRANSUE, EMILY R.
On Call
St. Martin's
Patients help educate a new doctor

WALKER, RICHARD
Encyclopedia of the Human Body
DK
Colorful guide to all our working parts

WERTH, BARRY
From Conception to Birth
Doubleday
Amazing views of human development

Planet Earth

ARTHUS-BERTHRAND, YANN
Earth From Above: 365 Days
Abrams
Portraits of natural and man-made beauty

BJORNERUD, MARCIA
*Reading the Rocks
Westview
Our planet's diary revealed

BLATT, HARVEY
*America's Environmental Report Card
MIT
Failing can lead to ecological disaster

BUCKLEY, BRUCE, EDWARD J. HOPKINS AND RICHARD WHITAKER
*Weather
Firefly
Understanding why it's always changing

COENRAADS, ROBERT R.
*Rocks & Fossils
Firefly
Providing keys to the Earth's past

DOHERTY, KIERAN
Marjory Stoneman Douglas
Twenty-First Century
Protector of the Everglades

GAUTHIER, GAIL
Saving the Planet and Stuff
Putnam's
A summer job, a crusade for Michael

LEUZZI, LINDA
Life Connections
Watts
Pioneers in ecology

MATTHEWS, ANNE
Wild Nights
North Point
Nature returns to the Big Apple

PATENT, DOROTHY HINSHAW
Shaping the Earth
Houghton Mifflin
Forces that formed our planet

PEARCE, FRED
*Deep Jungle
Eden Project
Exploring the world's rain forests

RENSHAW, AMANDA
Heaven & Earth
Phaidon
Worlds unseen by the naked eye

ROYTE, ELIZABETH
*Garbage Land
Little, Brown
Where the stuff you toss ends up

RYDEN, HOPE
Wildflowers Around the Year
Clarion
Skunk Cabbage to New York Ironweed

ST. ANTOINE, SARA
Stories from Where We Live
Milkweed
A celebration of the American prairie

ZEAMAN, JOHN
Overpopulation
Watts
A dangerous trend to ignore

The Way Things Work

ACZEL, AMIR D.
The Riddle of the Compass
Harvest
Who invented it?

BODANIS, DAVID
*Electric Universe
Crown
The invisible force that holds it all together

BRAIN, MARSHALL
Marshall Brain's More How Stuff Works
Wiley
From espresso machines to fusion bombs

GERSHENFELD, NEIL
*Fab
Basic
How to make (almost) anything

JONES, DAVID
*Mighty Robots
Annick
Mechanical marvels, past, present and future

KETTLEWELL, CAROLINE
Electric Dreams
Carroll & Graf
Teens build a car of the future

OWEN, DAVID
Copies in Seconds
Simon & Schuster
Inventing the Xerox machine

SULLIVAN, GEORGE
*Built to Last
Scholastic Nonfiction
Seventeen engineering marvels

Ancient Stones and Bones

BAHN, PAUL G.
Written in Bones
Firefly
Secrets of our distant past revealed

BURNIE, DAVID
The Concise Dinosaur Encyclopedia
Kingfisher
From the beginning to the age of mammals

DEEM, JAMES M.
*Bodies From the Ash
Houghton Mifflin
Life and death in ancient Pompeii

ELLISON, MICK
*Unearthing the Dragon
Pi Press
China's feathered dinosaurs

FARLOW, JAMES O.
Bringing Dinosaur Bones to Life
Watts
How we know what we know about dinosaurs

HAWASS, ZAHI
Curse of the Pharaohs
National Geographic
Adventures of an Egyptologist

OBREGÓN, MAURICIO
Beyond the Edge of the Sea
Modern Library
Real voyages remembered now in myth

STANLEY, DIANE
A Time Apart
Trophy
A Texas teen in an Iron Age community

TURNER, ALAN AND MARICIO ANTÓN
National Geographic Prehistoric Mammals
National Geographic
They ruled after the dinosaurs

WILCOX, CHARLOTTE
Mummies, Bones, & Body Parts
Carolrhoda
Human remains shed light on many cultures

*new book title

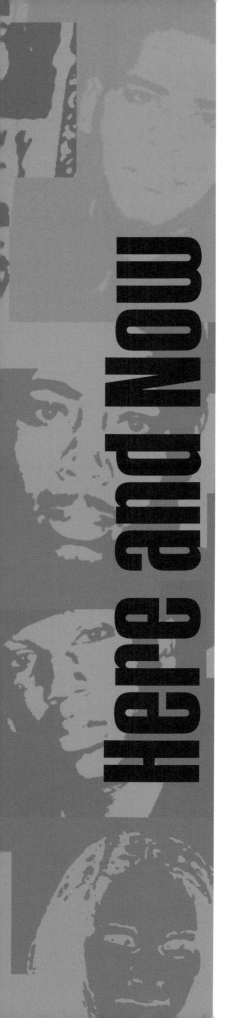

Here and Now

Do You Believe?

ABDUL-GHAFUR, SALEEMAH, EDITOR
*Living Islam Out Loud
Beacon
American Muslim women speak

COBBAN, HELENA
The Moral Architecture of World Peace
Univ. Pr. of Virginia
Conversations with 8 Nobel Laureates

GUEST, TIM
*My Life in Orange
Harcourt
Childhood on a New Age commune

MACK, STAN
The Story of the Jews
Jewish Lights
4,000 years in cartoons

MCCAIN, JOHN WITH MARK SALTER
Why Courage Matters
Random House
Finding the strength within yourself

MYERS, WALTER DEAN
A Time to Love
Scholastic
Faith tested beyond the ordinary

OLIVER, MARILYN TOWER
Muhammad
Lucent
The founder of Islam

O'NEILL, TERRY
Biomedical Ethics
Greenhaven
New technology brings troubling issues

PHILIP, NEIL
Mythology of the World
Kingfisher
Stories of civilizations, gods and heroes

RIESS, JANA
What Would Buffy Do?
Wiley
Leading viewers down spiritual paths

SIMONS, GARY, COMPILER
Be the Dream
Algonquin
Immigrants, inner-city youth, prep schools

STREISSGUTH, THOMAS
Utopian Visionaries
Oliver
Trying to create a perfect society

TEZUKA, OSAMU
Buddha: Volume 2, The Four Encounters
Vertical
More from the life of Siddhartha

WINSTON, DIANA
Wide Awake
Perigee
A Buddhist guide for teens

The Power of Words

BOYNTON, ROBERT S.
*The New New Journalism
Vintage
How 19 reporters get and tell their stories

BROOKS, TERRY
Sometimes the Magic Works
Del Rey
Inspiration from a master

CRAIG, STEVE
Sports Writing
Discover Writing
The game plan for a great article

DUNN, MARK
*Zounds!
St. Martin's Griffin
Other words to say when you don't know what to say

FRANK, STEVEN
The Pen Commandments
Pantheon
Unbreakable rules for better writing

JACKMAN, IAN, EDITOR
The Writer's Mentor
Random House
Advice from the world-famous writers

JACOB, IRIS
My Sisters' Voices
Holt
Teenage girls of color speak out

JONES, CAROLYN
Every Girl Tells a Story
Simon & Schuster
About her life, dreams, future

KALLAN, RICHARD
*Armed Gunmen, True Facts and Other Ridiculous Nonsense
Pantheon
Stupid idiots, cash money, deadly killers

LEVITHAN, DAVID, EDITOR
*Where We Are, What We See
Scholastic/Push
Words and images by teen writers and artists

MORRISON, LILLIAN, COMPILER
It Rained All Day That Night
August House
Sign the album with a rhyme

NIXON, JOAN LOWERY
The Making of a Writer
Delacorte
An author of mysteries shares tips

OTFINOSKI, STEVEN
*Extraordinary Short Story Writing
Scholastic
Creating great tales

QUINION, MICHAEL
Ballyhoo, Buckaroo, and Spuds
Smithsonian
Funny stories behind strange words

Getting It Together

Where We Are What We See

DAVID LEVITHAN, EDITOR
Push/Scholastic, 2005

Nightly Wonderland

As I lie in bed
the light through the window
hits one of the walls
and makes it look like another
doorway

The little girl in me
long since outgrown
wants to run to the secret passageway
and find my Wonderland, my Secret
Garden,
find my own special place

But the teenager currently residing here
cynical without reason
knows that if I jump out of bed —
probably stub my toe in the process —

if I come to that wall
if I reach out my hand
I'll just be disappointed

—Natalie Wright

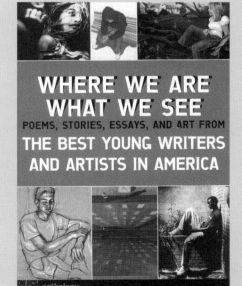

WHERE WE ARE WHAT WE SEE
POEMS, STORIES, ESSAYS, AND ART FROM
THE BEST YOUNG WRITERS AND ARTISTS IN AMERICA

WIATT, CARRIE AND BARBARA SCHROEDER
*The Diet for Teenagers Only
Regan
The healthy way to the body girls want

WILLIAMS, VENUS AND SERENA WILLIAMS WITH HILARY BEARD
*Venus & Serena: Serving From the Hip
Houghton Mifflin
Their ten rules for living, loving and winning

Crime and Justice

ABBOTT, GEOFFREY
The Executioner Always Chops Twice
St. Martin's
Putting criminals to death

ANGELICA, JADE CHRISTINE
We Are Not Alone
Haworth
Incest: disclosure through prosecution

BAYER, LINDA N.
Drugs, Crime, and Criminal Justice
Chelsea House
Past and present

BERGERON, DEB AND PAULA BREWER BYRON, EDITORS
From the Pain Come the Dream
Umbrage
Award-winning activists against injustice

BODE, JANET
Voices of Rape,
revised edition
Watts
Victims and rapists speak

CRAIG, EMILY
Teasing Secrets From the Dead
Crown
Infamous crime scene investigations

GOTTFRIED, TED
Homeland Security Versus Constitutional Rights
Twenty-First Century
Protecting our nation against terrorism
Should Drugs Be Legalized?
Twenty-First Century
Pro and con

HILLDORFER, JOSEPH AND ROBERT DUGONI
The Cyanide Canary
Free Press
Bringing a dangerous polluter to justice

HUBNER, JOHN
*Last Chance in Texas
Random House
Rehabilitating teenage lawbreakers

HYDE, MARGARET O. AND JOHN SETARO, M.D.
Drugs 101
Twenty-First Century
Consequences, current controversy, crime

JUNKIN, TIM
Bloodsworth
Algonquin
First death row inmate exonerated by DNA

ORR, TAMRA
Violence In Our Schools
Watts
Halls of hope, halls of fear

RODRÍGUEZ, JOSEPH
Juvenile
powerHouse
Images of what youthful offenders face

SALZMAN, MARK
True Notebooks
Knopf
Writings about life from juvenile hall

SPARGO, TAMSIN
Wanted Man
Bloomsbury
The wild tale of a dashing train robber

SUTTON, RANDY, COMPILER
True Blue
St. Martin's
What it means to be a cop

ZUGIBE, FREDERICK AND DAVID L. CARROLL
*Dissecting Death
Broadway
A medical examiner's most challenging cases

Looking Good

BIRD, EUGENIE
Fairie-ality
Candlewick
An adventure in fashion design

BROWN, BOBBI AND ANNEMARIE IVERSON
Bobbi Brown Teenage Beauty
Cliff Street
Appreciate what's special about you

CUNNINGHAM, MICHAEL AND GEORGE ALEXANDER
*Queens
Doubleday
Fabulous hairstyles of black women

DICKEY, A.
Hair Rules!
Villard
Good hair: kinky, curly, wavy

MASON, LINDA
Teen Makeup
Watson-Guptill
Looks to match your every mood

ODES, REBECCA; ESTHER DRILL AND HEATHER MCDONALD
The Looks Book
Penguin
Beauty: why, how and what style

SAMMONS, MARY BETH AND SAMANTHA MOSS
*Insparation
Watson-Guptill
Beauty boosters, stress zappers, spirit lifters

TRAIG, JENNIFER
Crafty Girl: Makeup
Chronicle
Do-it-yourself colors, your style

WARRICK, LEANNE
Hair Trix for Cool Chix
Watson-Guptill
TLC for all types of hair, for all girls

Love and Sex

BECKERMAN, MARTY
Generation S.L.U.T.
MTV Books/Pocket
Statistics, exaggerations, lies and truth

BODE, JANET AND STAN MACK
Heartbreak and Roses,
revised edition
Watts
True stories of troubled love

BRYNIE, FAITH HICKMAN
101 Questions About Sex and Sexuality
Twenty-First Century
All the answers you've been looking for

BURGESS, MELVIN
Doing It
Henry Holt
The truth behind the "player's talk"

CLAUSNER-PETIT, MAGALI WITH MELISSA DALY
Sex Explained
Amulet
Your guide to the birds and bees

DOMITRZ, MICHAEL J.
May I Kiss You?
Awareness
When it is okay, and when it is not

LINDSAY, JEANNE WARREN
Teen Dads,
revised edition
Morning Glory
Supporting your partner and child

MADARAS, LYNDA
The "What's Happening to My Body?" Book for Boys,
3rd edition
Newmarket
Answers to often-embarrassing questions

The "What's Happening to My Body?" Book for Girls,
3rd edition
Newmarket
Your transformation to womanhood

NAIK, ANITA
Flirtology
Razorbill
Girls, flirting tips to win guys

YOUNG, CATHY
One Hot Second
Knopf
Stories about desire

LGBTQ: Being Gay

BOYER, DAVID
***Kings & Queens**
Soft Skull
Celebrating the big night queer style

HOWE, JAMES
***Totally Joe**
Atheneum
13, chronicling his life, baring his soul

HUEGEL, KELLY
GLBTQ
Free Spirit
Queer and questioning survival guide

JOHNSON, MAUREEN
***The Bermudez Triangle**
Razorbill
Mel and Avery: best friends, hooking up

KANTROWITZ, ARNIE
***Walt Whitman**
Chelsea House
19th Century trailblazing writer

LAROCHELLE, DAVID
***Absolutely, Positively Not...**
Arthur A. Levine
Steven, ignoring the painfully obvious

LEVITHAN, DAVID
Boy Meets Boy
Knopf
Boy loses boy, drama ensues, boy gets boy

MCCANN, RICHARD
***Mother of Sorrows**
Pantheon
Stories of obsession, rejection, survival

MYRACLE, LAUREN
Kissing Kate
Dutton
Lissa realizing she can't be just friends

PETERS, JULIE ANNE
***Far From Xanadu**
Little, Brown
Mike, falling for the new girl in town

RACHEL, T. COLE AND RITA D. COSTELLO, EDITORS
***Bend, Don't Shatter**
Red Rattle/Soft Skull
Sweetness, sadness, love, desire in verse

RUDACILLE, DEBORAH
***The Riddle of Gender**
Pantheon
Science and history of transgendered lives

SANCHEZ, ALEX
***Rainbow Road**
Simon & Schuster
3 friends, 1 journey across the country

SELVADURAI, SHYAM
***Swimming in the Monsoon Sea**
Tundra
Shunned by his family, falling for a boy

SLOAN, BRIAN
***A Really Nice Prom Mess**
Simon & Schuster
Cam and Shane's thwarted evening out

TRACHTENBERG, ROBERT, EDITOR
***When I Knew**
Regan
Coming out in their own words

WYETH, SHARON DENNIS
Orphea Proud
Delacorte
Discovering herself at the mike

The Changing Scene

ALMOND, STEVE
Candyfreak
Algonquin
The chocolate underbelly of America

BAMBERGER, MICHAEL
Wonderland
Atlantic Monthly
Senior year and an over the top prom

BOTHA, TED
Mongo
Bloomsbury
Treasures in the trash

CHAPLIN, HEATHER AND AARON RUBY
***Smartbomb**
Algonquin
An insider's look at the gaming world

GARCIA, BOBBITO
Where'd You Get Those?
Testify
Talking about sneakers in NYC

Far From Xanadu

JULIE ANNE PETERS
Megan Tingley Books/Little, Brown and Company, 2005

She raised her eyes to mine and we melded together. I could feel it. Her chest heaved and she expelled an audible sigh. "God." She lowered her chin to her chest. "I am so lost here. So out of my realm."

I'll help you find your realm, I thought. I'll ride you to the castle on a tall white steed and slay every dragon in your path.

"I guess you know my name." She tilted her head up and crossed her eyes at me. "I'm sure the whole school does by now. What's yours?"

"Mike." I cleared my windpipe.

"Mike." She bumped my shoulder with hers. Coy. Flirty. God, give me strength. It was suddenly a hundred and ten degrees in here.

"'Scuse me," I stammered. Setting my cleats back on the shelf, I pulled my sweatshirt over my head and hung it on the hook in my locker. When I turned back, she was staring at me. And not at my face.

"Sorry," she said, her jaw slack. "I... I thought you were a guy."

"Yeah." I tried to smile, but the smile twisted, like my stomach. "I, uh, get that a lot."

Far from Xanadu

Teacher Man

BY FRANK MCCOURT
Scribner, 2005

In every class there's a pest put on earth to test you. He usually sits in the last row, where he can tilt his chair against the wall. You've already talked to the class about the danger of tilting: Chair could slip, children, and you could be hurt. Then teacher has to write a report in case parents complain or threaten to sue.

Andrew knows the tilting chair will annoy you, at least get your attention. Then he can play the little game that will catch the.eyes of the girls. You'll say. Hey, Andrew.

He'll take his time. This is a showdown, man, and girls are watching.

Wha'?

That is the teenage sound you won't find in a dictionary. Wha'? Parents hear it constantly. It means, Whaddya want? Why you bothering me?

The chair, Andrew. Would you put it down, please?

I'm just sittin' minding my own business.

The chair, Andrew, has four legs. Tilting on two legs could cause an accident.

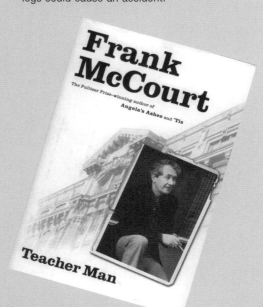

GROSS, MICHAEL JOSEPH
Starstruck
Bloomsbury
Trailing fans, chasing celebrities

KILPATRICK, NANCY
The Goth Bible
St. Martin's Griffin
Death, darkness and Doc Martens

KYI, TANYA LLOYD
The Blue Jean Book
Annick
History of a fashion staple

NELSON, ASHLEY
The Combination
Red Rattle/Soft Skull
Oral history of a New Orleans neighborhood

PIAZZA, TOM
Why New Orleans Matters
Regan
The city, before and after a hurricane

PLETKA, BOB
My So-Called Digital Life
Santa Monica
2,000 teens, 300 cameras, 30 days of images

VISE, DAVID A. AND MARK MALSEED
The Google Story
Delacorte
Inside one of today's media giants

Make up Your Mind

LASSIEUR, ALLISON
Abortion
Lucent
A current discussion of these issues

LEVY, ARIEL
Female Chauvinist Pigs
Free
Like one of the guys or just outrageous

MORAN, MARK AND MARK SCEURMAN
Weird U.S.
Barnes & Noble
America's legends and best kept secrets

QUART, ALISSA
Branded
Perseus
Teens: manipulated by the media?

SINGER, MARILYN, EDITOR
Face Relations
Simon & Schuster
Stories of youth embracing diversity

Overcoming Odds

ABEEL, SAMANTHA
My Thirteenth Winter
Orchard
Enduring a math disability

DAVIS, DEBORAH, EDITOR
You Look Too Young to be a Mom
Perigee
Teen mothers speak out

FEARNELEY, FRAN, EDITOR
I Wrote on All Four Walls
Annick
Teens speaking out on violence

FISHER, ANTWONE QUENTON AND MIM EICHLER RIVAS
Finding Fish
Morrow
An abandoned boy finding himself

HUGHES, LYNNE B.
You Are Not Alone
Scholastic
Healing after a parent dies

KELLER, HELEN
The Story of My Life, the restored edition
Modern Library
The challenge of being deaf and blind

LEHMAN, CAROLYN
Strong at the Heart
Farrar, Straus and Giroux
Surviving childhood sexual abuse

LOUISE, REGINA
Somebody's Someone
Warner
Looking for her own loving family

MISHLER, WILLIAM
A Measure of Endurance
Knopf
When Steven, 16, lost his arms

RUNYON, BRENT
The Burn Journals
Knopf
14 and attempting suicide

SIANA, JOLENE
Go Ask Ogre
Process Books
Words and images from a suicidal cutter

SUMMER, LAURALEE
Learning Joy from Dogs Without Collars
Simon & Schuster
From homeless shelters to Harvard

SWADOS, ELIZABETH
My Depression
Hyperion
The composer's portrait of her illness

Remarkable People

War and Peace

Genius

BY MARFÉ FERGUSON DELANO

National Geographic Society, 2005

ALBERT EINSTEIN MIGHT HAVE SMILED at the title of this book. He found it amusing that people considered him a genius. Although he was proud of his achievements, he saw himself as just an ordinary person. In fact, he once said, "I have no special talents. I am only passionately curious." Yet if anyone deserves to be labeled a genius, it is Albert Einstein. His ideas not only laid the path for much of 20th-century science, they remain vital to science in this century as well. His masterpiece, called the general theory of relativity, brought him worldwide fame. It also transformed our everyday ideas of time and space and the way the universe works.

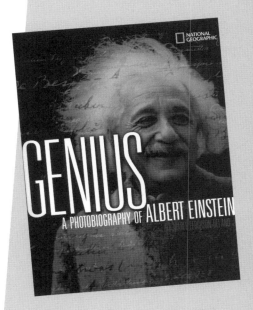

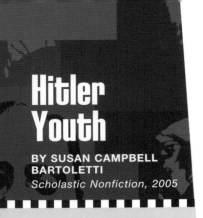

Hitler Youth

BY SUSAN CAMPBELL BARTOLETTI
Scholastic Nonfiction, 2005

Some parents tried in vain to discourage their children from joining. "Father tried to ram into me that there was no glory nor heroism in war and battle," said Henry Metelmann. "Only madness, desperation, fright, and unbelievable brutality."

Despite his father's warnings, Henry found himself drawn to the Hitler Youth. "I was carried away by it all," he said. "It did not take me long before I wore the striking uniform of the Hitler Youth.... I could only promise my father that I would think about what he had told me."

It was the same for the five Scholl brothers and sisters. "We entered into the Hitler Youth with body and soul," said Inge Scholl, the oldest. "And we could not understand why our father did not approve, why he was not happy and proud.... Sometimes he would compare Hitler with the Pied Piper of Hamelin, who, with his flute, led the children to destruction."

HITLER YOUTH
GROWING UP IN HITLER'S SHADOW
SUSAN CAMPBELL BARTOLETTI

EXUM, ANDREW
This Man's Army
Gotham
Fighting al-Qaeda in Afghanistan

GOTTFRIED, TED
The Great Fatherland War
Twenty-First Century
The rise and fall of the Soviet Union

GRABER, JANET
***Resistance**
Marshall Cavendish
Marianne, helping to defeat the Germans

HAMANN, JACK
***On American Soil**
Algonquin
Justice denied to cover our shame

HEDIN, ROBERT, EDITOR
Old Glory
Persea
Heroism and horror of war in poetry

HEFFERNAN, COLLEEN
***A Kind of Courage**
Orca
David, a conscientious objector during WWI

KOFF, CLEA
The Bone Woman
Random House
Searching for truth in mass graves

LIPSKY, DAVID
Absolutely American
Houghton Mifflin
Four years, the West Point experience

MAZER, HARRY
***Heroes Don't Run**
Simon & Schuster
Adam enlisting to honor his father

MCBRIDE, JAMES
Miracle at St. Anna
Riverhead
WWII: The Buffalo Soldiers' heroism in Italy

MORPURGO, MICHAEL
Private Peaceful
Scholastic
At 14, following his brother into battle

MYERS, WALTER DEAN
Patrol
HarperCollins
A poem of a young soldier in Vietnam

NELSON, PETE
Left for Dead
Delacorte
Teen seeks justice for a US Navy captain

O'DONNELL, JOE
***Japan 1945**
Vanderbilt Univ.
Photos from a Marine's private collection

OTSUKA, JULIE
When the Emperor Was Divine
Knopf
Japanese Americans sent to a desert camp

PHILLIPS, MICHAEL M.
***The Gift of Valor**
Broadway
A Marine's sacrifice during the Iraqi War

SALISBURY, GRAHAM
***Eyes of the Emperor**
Wendy Lamb
WWII: Eddy, a target to train attack dogs

SPILLEBEEN, GEERT
***Kipling's Choice**
Houghton Mifflin
A father's dream of war, a son's reality

UNG, LOUNG
***Lucky Child**
HarperCollins
One who left Cambodia to live in the USA

WILLIAMS, BUZZ
Spare Parts
Gotham
Marine reservist sent to the Persian Gulf

WULFFSON, DON
Soldier X.
Viking
Fighting in a war he doesn't believe in

Working

ALBRECHT, KAT WITH JANA MURPHY
The Lost Pet Chronicles
Bloomsbury
K-9 cop turned pet detective

CODELL, ESMÉ RAJI
Educating Esmé
Algonquin
The diary of a teacher's first year

ESQUITH, RAFE
There Are No Shortcuts
Pantheon
An award-winning teacher speaks

GREEN, MELISSA FAY
Last Man Out
Harcourt
Facing death in a Nova Scotia coal mine

HAINES, LURENE
The Writer's Guide to the Business of Comics
Watson-Guptill
Tips from industry insiders

HAN, PETER
***Nobodies to Somebodies**
Portfolio
How great careers got started

JACKSON, DONNA M.
***ER Vets**
Houghton Mifflin
Devoted to saving animals' lives

KENIG, GRACIELA
Best Careers for Bilingual Latinos
VGM
Are you fluent in Spanish and English?

MOREM, SUSAN
*101 Tips for Graduates
Ferguson
Skills for moving from student to worker

ROBERTS-DAVIS, TANYA
We Need to Go to School
Groundwood
Nepalese child carpet workers

SCHIFF, NANCY RICA
Odd Jobs
Ten Speed
Working in peculiar occupations

SCHWAGER, TINA AND MICHELE SCHUERGER
Cool Women, Hot Jobs
Free Spirit
Tips for teens

UNGER, ZAC
Working Fire
Penguin
The making of an accidental fireman

ZANNOS, SUSAN
Careers in Education
Mitchell Lane
Latinos at work

Never Again: The Holocaust

BARTOLETTI, SUSAN CAMPBELL
*Hitler Youth
Scholastic
Growing up in the shadows of a dictator

BLEIER, INGE JOSEPH AND DAVID E. GUMPERT
Inge
William B. Eerdmans
Her journey through Nazi Europe

CHOTJEWITZ, DAVID
Daniel Half Human and the Good Nazi
Atheneum
Best friends torn apart by anti-Semitism

CROCI, PASCAL
Auschwitz
Abrams
Horrors of the camp in a graphic novel

DENENBERG, BARRY
*Shadow Life
Scholastic
A fresh view of Anne Frank's world

FRANK, ANNE
The Diary of a Young Girl,
definitive edition
Doubleday
Her innermost feelings from her hiding place

GESSEN, MASHA
Ester and Ruzya
Dial
Grandmothers reliving Russia's history

GIBLIN, JAMES CROSS
The Life and Death of Adolf Hitler
Clarion
Portrait of a 20th-century dictator

HILLMAN, LAURA
*I Will Plant You a Lilac Tree
Atheneum
A memoir of an Schindler's List survivor

LOWENSTEIN, SALLIE
*Waiting for Eugene
Lion Stone
Drawing her father's war-time memories

ROGASKY, BARBARA
Smoke and Ashes,
Revised and Expanded Ed.
Holiday House
A history in words and images

SPIEGELMAN, ART
Maus: A Survivor's Tale, I and II
Pantheon
An artist's look at the death camps

STILLMAN, LARRY
A Match Made in Hell
Univ. of Wisconsin
True story: a Jewish boy and an outlaw

WIESEL, ELIE
After the Darkness
Schocken
Surviving the horror and bearing witness

Women

BAUSUM, ANN
With Courage and Cloth
National Geographic
The fight for the right to vote

BOHANNON, LISA FREDERIKSEN
Woman's Work
Morgan Reynolds
Betty Friedan and women's rights

BOLDEN, TONYA
33 Things Every Girl Should Know About Women's History
Crown
From suffragettes to the E.R.A.

COLMAN, PENNY
Girls
Scholastic
Growing up female in America

COON, NORA E., EDITOR AND COMPILER
It's Your Rite
Beyond Words
Today's girls speak: coming-of-age

DEAK, ERZSI AND KRISTIN EMBRY LITCHMAN, EDITORS
Period Pieces
HarperCollins
Girls on the verge of womanhood

GAINES, ANN
Coco Chanel
Chelsea House
The revolutionary fashion designer

GRUNWALD, LISA AND STEPHEN J. ADLER
*Women's Letters
Dial
The female perspective on American history

GUERRILLA GIRLS, THE
Bitches, Bimbos, and Ballbreakers
Penguin
A guide to female stereotypes

HARRISON, SABRINA WARD
Brave on the Rocks
Villard
An artist's intimate journey

KENSCHAFT, LORI
Lydia Maria Child
Oxford University Press
Her quest for racial justice

LESTER, JOAN STEINAU
Fire in My Soul
Atria
Eleanor Holmes Norton, political pioneer

LEWIS, J. PATRICK, WITH ILLUSTRATIONS BY MARK SUMMERS
*Vherses
Creative Editions
Poems and portraits of triumph

MAURER, RICHARD
The Wright Sister
Roaring Brook
The woman behind the famous men

NAM, VICKIE
Yell-Oh Girls!
Quill
Asian Americans speaking up

SULLIVAN, OTHA RICHARD
African American Women Scientists & Inventors
Wiley
Black stars present and past

VAN PELT, LORI
*Amelia Earhart
Forge
The world's best known aviatrix

ZUKERMAN, EUGENIA
In My Mother's Closet
Sorin
Daughters remembering

Mother of the Dance

Face white death mask

Mouth a slash of red

Cheekbones sculpted stone

She moves to move

Like something said

A phantom bending

Bone to bone

TREMBLE

spAsm

sudden

f

a

l

l

Delirium

The glance

Stark fantasy

In angles called

The Mother of the Dance.

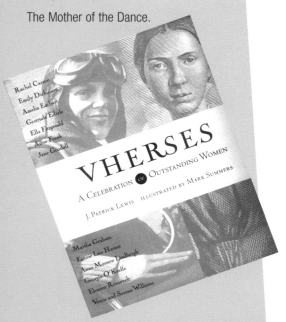

Memoir

APPELT, KATHI
My Father's Summers
Henry Holt
Coming of age in an imperfect
family

BROKAW, TOM
A Long Way From Home
Random House
The broadcaster's youth in
South Dakota

CHILDERS, MARY
*Welfare Brat
Bloomsbury
Battling her mom in 1960's
Bronx

CONLON-MCIVOR, MAURA
FBI Girl
Warner
Deciphering her father's
secrets

CRUTCHER, CHRIS
King of the Mild Frontier
Greenwillow
Growing up to become an
author

DUDMAN, MARTHA TOD
Expecting to Fly
Simon & Schuster
Surviving the turbulent sixties

GANTOS, JACK
Hole in My Life
Farrar, Straus and Giroux
A famous author's prison
experience

MCCOURT, FRANK
*Teacher Man
Scribner
30 years: 5 days a week, 5
periods a day

MOEHRINGER, J.R.
*The Tender Bar
Hyperion
Role models in unexpected places

MYERS, WALTER DEAN
Bad Boy
HarperCollins
A favorite writer's critical Harlem
years

PATCHETT, ANN
Truth & Beauty
HarperCollins
A powerful friendship between
two writers

PECK, ROBERT NEWTON
*Weeds in Bloom
Random House
Plain folk shaping an
extraordinary author

POWERS, KEMP
*The Shooting
Thunder's Mouth
Killing a best friend: an
atonement

SCHEERES, JULIA
*Jesus Land
Counterpoint
Race, adoption, rebellion and
family

STING
Broken Music
Dial
Autobiography of a pop icon

STRINGER, LEE
Sleepaway School
Seven Stories
Surviving racism, abuse and
poverty

WALLS, JEANNETTE
*The Glass Castle
Scribner
Unconditional love in a
dysfunctional family

*new book title

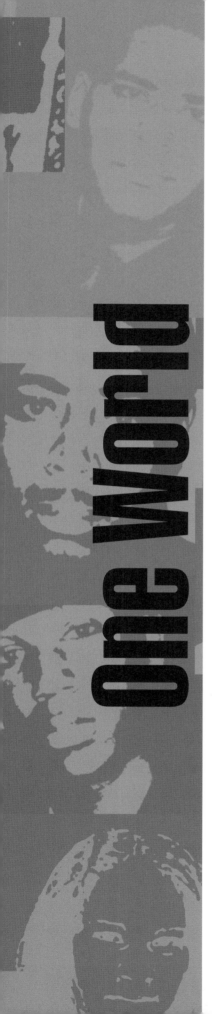

One World

Africa

ADICHIE, CHIMAMANDA NGOZI
Purple Hibiscus
Algonquin
Lives shattered under a military coup

BEARD, PETER
Zara's Tales
Knopf
Adventures with wildlife in Kenya

DIALLO, KADIATOU AND CRAIG WOLFF
My Heart Will Cross This Ocean
One World
Remembering her son Amadou and more

DIRIE, WARIS
Desert Flower
Ariel
Escaping Somalia's harsh traditions

DONGALA, EMMANUEL
***Johnny Mad Dog**
Farrar, Straus and Giroux
Two teens in the chaos of civil war

EMECHETA, BUCHI
The Bride Price
George Braziller
An Ibo girl's ill-fated love

FARMER, NANCY
A Girl Named Disaster
Orchard
On a harrowing journey to Zimbabwe

IWEALA, UZODINMA
***Beasts of No Nation**
HarperCollins
Agu, a boy forced to be a soldier

KURTZ, JANE, EDITOR
Memories of Sun
Amistad/Greenwillow
Stories of growing up African today

LAINÉ, DANIEL AND PIERRE ALEXANDRE
African Kings
Ten Speed
Vivid portraits of tribal royalty

LEKUTON, JOSEPH LEMASOLAI WITH HERMAN VIOLA
Facing the Lion
National Geographic
Growing up Maasai on the Kenyan savanna

MAFUNDIKWA, SAKI
Afrikan Alphabets
Mark Batty
Writing systems as culture and art

MATHABANE, MIRIAM AS TOLD TO MARK MATHABANE
Miriam's Song
Simon & Schuster
Growing up oppressed in South Africa

MCCALL SMITH, ALEXANDER
The Girl Who Married a Lion and Other Tales from Africa
Pantheon
Folktales from Zimbabwe and Botswana

NAIDOO, BEVERLEY
Out of Bounds
HarperCollins
Seven stories of South African lives

NAZER, MENDE AND DAMIEN LEWIS
Slave
PublicAffairs
Seized from her Sudanese village at 12

PATON, ALAN
Cry, the Beloved Country
Scribner's
A Zulu parson in search of his son

REEF, CATHERINE
This Our Dark Country
Clarion
Liberia, its ongoing, troubled history

STRATTON, ALLAN
Chanda's Secrets
Annick
Dreams of the future as death takes hold

TADJO, VÉRONIQUE, EDITOR
Talking Drums
Bloomsbury
Introducing poems from the continent

WHELAN, GLORIA
***Listening for Lions**
HarperCollins
Rachel, orphaned in East Africa, 1919

The Middle East

ABU-JABER, DIANA
***The Language of Baklava**
Pantheon
A feast of Jordanian memories

GALLEGO GARCÍA, LAURA
***The Legend of the Wandering King**
Arthur A. Levine
A prince who loved poetry in 6th C. Arabia

GREENFELD, HOWARD
***A Promise Fulfilled**
Greenwillow
The creation of a Jewish state

HAKAKIAN, ROYA
Journey from the Land of No
Crown
Coming of age as revolution sweeps Iran

MOAVENI, AZADEH
***Lipstick Jihad**
PublicAffairs
Reclaiming her heritage in Tehran

NYE, NAOMI SHIHAB
19 Varieties of Gazelle
Greenwillow
Treasured memories of a homeland in poems

SALEEM, HINER
***My Father's Rifle**
Farrar, Straus and Giroux
Growing up as Saddam threatens the Kurds

SATRAPI, MARJANE
Persepolis
Pantheon
A childhood in Iran: a graphic novel
Persepolis 2
Pantheon
A young rebel finding her place

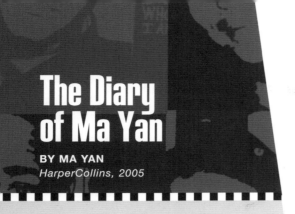

The Diary of Ma Yan

BY MA YAN
HarperCollins, 2005

We have a week of vacation. Mother takes me aside.

"My child. There's something I have to tell you."

I answer, "Mother, if you have something to tell me, do it quickly. Tell me."

But her words are like a death sentence.

"I'm afraid you may have been to school for the last time."

My eyes go wide. I look up at her. "How can you say something like that? These days you can't live without an education. Even a peasant needs knowledge to ensure good harvests and to farm well."

Mother insists. "Your brothers and you add up to three children to be sent to school. Your father is the only one earning money, and it's not enough."

I'm frightened. "Does this mean I have to come home to work?" "Yes."

"And my two brothers?"

"Your two brothers will carry on with their studies"

I protest. "Why can boys study and not girls?"

Her smile is tired. "You're still liittle.When you grow up, you'll understand."

SOUAD
Burned Alive
Warner
When a girl breaks the rules in Palestine

STEIN, TAMMAR
***Light Years**
Knopf
Maya, haunted by her Israeli past

Asia

AKBAR, SAID HYDER AND SUSAN BURTON
***Come Back to Afghanistan**
Bloomsbury
California teen in his parents' homeland

AOKI, SHOICHI
***Fresh Fruits**
Phaidon
Tokyo teens dressed Harajuku style

CAREY, PETER
***Wrong About Japan**
Knopf
Exploring the culture with his son

DAI, SIJIE
Balzac and the Little Chinese Seamstress
Knopf
2 boys telling tales from forbidden books

DELISLE, GUY
***Pyongyang**
Drawn & Quarterly
A graphic journey in North Korea

FREEDMAN, RUSSELL
Confucius
Arthur A. Levine
Philosopher, educator, diplomat

HAQ, HINA
Sadika's Way
Academy Chicago
How tradition rules her life in Pakistan

HOOBLER, DOROTHY & THOMAS HOOBLER
***The Sword that Cut the Burning Grass**
Philomel
A samurai apprentice's dangerous mission

HOSSEINI, KHALED
The Kite Runner
Riverhead
Amir and Hassan: friends in Kabul

KOUL, SUDHA
The Tiger Ladies
Beacon
Memories of Kashmir, a "Paradise on Earth"

LIU, SIYU AND OREL PROTOPOPESCU
A Thousand Peaks
Pacific View
Introducing the poetry of China

MA, YAN
***The Diary of Ma Yan**
HarperCollins
The struggles of a Chinese schoolgirl

MAJOR, JOHN AND BETTY J. BELANUS
Caravan to America
Cricket
8 who practice the arts of the Silk Road

MIN, ANCHEE
Wild Ginger
Houghton Mifflin
Two girls in love with the same boy

NAMU, YANG ERCHE AND CHRISTINE MATHIEU
Leaving Mother Lake
Little, Brown
A singer looks back at a Chinese girlhood

NAPOLI, DONNA JO
Bound
Atheneum
Xing Xing, a Chinese Cinderella's story

PARK, LINDA SUE
When My Name Was Keoko
Clarion
Korea, occupied by the Japanese military

PAZIRA, NELOFER
***A Bed of Red Flowers**
Free
Her life in war-torn Afghanistan

PERKINS, MITALI
Monsoon Summer
Delacorte
The lessons India teaches to Jazz

SEE, LISA
***Snow Flower and the Secret Fan**
Random House
Female friendship tested in rural China

SHEN, FAN
***Gang of One**
Univ. of Nebraska
Coming of age in Communist China

STAPLES, SUZANNE FISHER
***Under the Persimmon Tree**
Frances Foster
An Afghan girl fleeing the Taliban

STINE, CATHERINE
***Refugees**
Delacorte
Learning about loss in Pakistan and NYC

SUE, CHUN
Beijing Doll
Riverhead
Sex life of a Chinese rock and roller

TALARIGO, JEFF
The Pearl Diver
Nan A. Talese
How leprosy shattered her life

TOER, PRAMOEDYA ANANTA
All That is Gone
Hyperion
Suffering and survival in Indonesia

TORTAJADA, ANA
The Silenced Cry
Thomas Dunne
A diary, a journey to Afghanistan

UNG, LOUNG
First They Killed My Father
HarperCollins
A daughter's memories of Cambodia

WHELAN, GLORIA
Chu Ju's House
HarperCollins
A girl torn from her Chinese family

YU, CHUN
***Little Green**
Simon & Schuster
A child's view of the Cultural Revolution

Europe

ALMOND, DAVID
Counting Stars
Delacorte
18 Stories recalling a writer's life

ARONSON, MARC
Sir Walter Ralegh and the Quest for El Dorado
Clarion
From the English court to the New World

BARTOLETTI, SUSAN CAMPBELL
Black Potatoes
Houghton Mifflin
The story of the Great Irish Famine

BOLOGNESE, DON
The Warhorse
Simon & Schuster
Lorenzo, 15, a Renaissance hero

BRESLIN, THERESA
Remembrance
Delacorte
Five Scottish lives changed by WWI

CADNUM, MICHAEL
Daughter of the Wind
Orchard
Hallgerd, a Viking girl kidnapped

CASTELLANI, CHRISTOPHER
A Kiss From Maddalena
Algonquin
Longing for love in war-torn Italy

CERVANTES, MIGUEL DE
...Don Quixote de la Mancha; Charles Jarvis, translator
Oxford Univ. Pr.
A dreamer of impossible dreams

CHARLESWORTH, MONIQUE
The Children's War
Knopf
Ilse and Nicolai, living through WWII

CHEVALIER, TRACY
The Lady and the Unicorn
Dutton
Tales hidden in medieval tapestries

CORNWELL, BERNARD
The Archer's Tale
HarperCollins
Seeking revenge with a bow and arrow

GIFF, PATRICIA REILLY
Nory Ryan's Song
Delacorte
Helping her family survive the famine

GOTTFRIED, TED
The Cold War
Twenty-First Century
Soviet politics and collapse

HAUTZIG, ESTHER
The Endless Steppe
HarperCollins
Growing up in Siberia

HAWES, LOUISE
The Vanishing Point
Houghton Mifflin
Vini's emergence as a 16th c. painter

HEUSTON, KIMBERLEY
Dante's Daughter
Front Street
Antonia's journey with her famous father

HOOPER, MARY
Petals in the Ashes
Bloomsbury
Hannah facing horror: the Great Fire, 1666

LEVINSON, NANCY SMILER
Magellan
Clarion
Attempting to sail around the world

MEYER, CAROLYN
Doomed Queen Anne
Gulliver
Losing the affection of Henry VIII

MORGAN, NICOLA
Fleshmarket
Delacorte
1822: Dr. Knox, healer or murderer?

O'CONNOR, JOSEPH
Star of the Sea
Harcourt
Trapped on a ship with a killer

ORCZY, EMMUSKA
The Scarlet Pimpernel
Pocketbook
Rescuing nobility from the Terrorists

SHAWCROSS, WILLIAM
Queen and Country
Simon & Schuster
The fifty-year reign of Elizabeth II

SIMOEN, JAN
What About Anna?
Walker
Searching Bosnia for her missing brother

SIMON, SCOTT
***Pretty Birds**
Random House
She is 17 and a sniper in Sarajevo

THAL, LILLI
***Mimus**
Annick
War and betrayal in a medieval kingdom

The Story of My Life

BY FARAH AHMEDI WITH TAMIM ANSARY

Simon Spotlight Entertainment, 2005

ALYCE WANTED ME TO SHARE THE STORY OF MY LIFE.

I told her that I wasn't ready, that it was too soon. I'm not even nineteen years old, and I haven't achieved anything yet. But Alyce said that with a life like mine, surviving itself is an achievement—just surviving.

I don't know if she's right. When I look back at my childhood in Afghanistan, it seems so far away and long ago. Back then I thought I would grow up and grow old in the city of Kabul, surrounded by my big, complicated, loving family. Little did I know I would lose most of them before I turned fourteen.

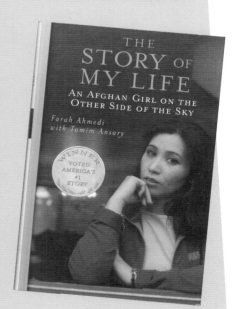

THE STORY OF MY LIFE
AN AFGHAN GIRL ON THE OTHER SIDE OF THE SKY
Farah Ahmedi with Tamim Ansary

WINNER VOTED AMERICA'S #1 STORY

THOMAS, JANE RESH
*The Counterfeit Princess
Clarion
A teen spy in England's royal Tudor court

TURNBULL, ANN
No Shame, No Fear
Candlewick
Love despite religious differences

WATSON, ELSA
Maid Marian
Crown
Intrigue and romance in medieval England

WHITELAW, NANCY
*Catherine the Great and the Enlightenment in Russia
Morgan Reynolds
A powerful and passionate ruler

Native Americans

BRUCHAC, JOSEPH
*At the End of Ridge Road
Milkweed
Memoir of the writer's Abenaki roots
Pocahontas
Harcourt
The willful girl bringing peace

CARDOZA, CHRISTOPHER
*Edward S. Curtis: The Women
Bulfinch
Portraits that honor spirit and tradition

CARLSON, LORI MARIE, EDITOR
*Moccasin Thunder
HarperCollins
Powerful stories of today's Indian teens

CARVELL, MARLENE
Who Will Tell My Brother?
Hyperion
School mascot: pride and prejudice

COLTON, LARRY
Counting Coup
Warner
Girls' basketball on the Little Big Horn

FREEDMAN, RUSSELL
The Life and Death of Crazy Horse
Holiday House
A warrior of courage and passion

KATZ, WILLIAM LOREN
Black Indians
Aladdin
A hidden heritage

LISLE, JANET TAYLOR
The Crying Rocks
Simon & Schuster
Joelle, meeting the ghosts of her past

MCMASTER, GERALD AND CLIFFORD E. TRAFZER, EDITORS
Native Universe
National Museum of the American Indian, Smithsonian Institution/ National Geographic
Art and culture of indigenous peoples

OCHOA, ANNETTE PIÑA; BETSY FRANCO, AND TRACI L. GOURDINE, EDITORS
Night is Gone, Day is Still Coming
Candlewick
Stories and poems by teens and young adults

PHILIP, NEIL, EDITOR
In a Sacred Manner I Live
Clarion
Looking at life with wisdom

REES, CELIA
Sorceress
Candlewick
Agnes and Mary, linked across centuries

RIDDLE, PAXTON
The Education of Ruby Loonfoot
Five Star
A conflict of cultures for an Objibwe girl

ROBINSON, EDEN
Monkey Beach
Houghton Mifflin
Spirits assist Lisamarie in this life

SMITH, ROLAND
The Last Lobo
Hyperion
Jake tries to save a wolf on the Hopi Rez

SMITH, WILLIAM JAY
The Cherokee Lottery
Curbstone
A shameful part of U.S. history in verse

STEVENS, MARCUS
Useful Girl
Algonquin
A journey to honor the past and find love

SULLIVAN, PAUL
Maata's Journal
Atheneum
An Inuit girl facing change in the Arctic

VIOLA, HERMAN J.
Warrior Artists
National Geographic
Recording their lives and loss of freedom

WALDMAN, NEIL
Wounded Knee
Atheneum
"A people's dream died there." Black Elk

The Americas

CAMERON, ANN
Colibri
Farrar, Straus and Giroux
Kidnapped in Guatemala to help a beggar

DE LA GARZA, BEATRICE
Pillars of Gold and Silver
Piñata
Bianca's new home in Mexico

FALCONER, COLIN
Feathered Serpent
Three Rivers
Cortes' Aztec translator and lover

GOODMAN, JOAN ELIZABETH
Paradise
Houghton Mifflin
Lovers, stranded on a Canadian island

HERRERA, JUAN FELIPE
Thunderweavers
Univ. of Arizona Pr.
Bilingual poems of the violence in Chiapas

MARTEL, SUZANNE
The King's Daughter
Groundwood
Wed to a stranger in Canada's wilderness

MONTEJO, VICTOR
Popol Vuh
Groundwood
The Maya-from creation to conquest

PAULSEN, GARY
The Crossing
Orchard
Manuel, in flight from Mexico to Texas

WHYMAN, MATT
*Boy Kills Man
HarperTempest
Alberto: teen drug dealer in Colombia

WISEMAN, EVA
A Place Not Home
Stoddart Kids
Escaping from Hungary to Canada

WOOD, FRANCES M.
Daughter of Madrugada
Delacorte
When Mexico lost California

WOOD, MICHAEL
Conquistadors
University of California Press
Spanish explorers in the New World

YEE, PAUL
Dead Man's Gold and Other Stories
Groundwood
Ten tales of relocating to North America

Latinos

ABRAHAM, SUSAN GONZALES AND DENISE GONZALES ABRAHAM
*Surprising Cecilia
Cinco Puntos
On to high school in the Rio Grande Valley

ALVAREZ, JULIA
Finding Miracles
Knopf
Milly, exploring her roots

BIERHORST, JOHN, EDITOR
Latin American Folktales
Pantheon
From Hispanic and Indian traditions

CANALES, VIOLA
*The Tequila Worm
Wendy Lamb
Sofia, growing up in a Texas barrio

CARLSON, LORI MARIE, EDITOR
*Red Hot Salsa
Henry Holt
Bilingual poems celebrating youth

DÍAZ, JUNOT
Drown
Riverhead
Stories of Dominican youth

MARTINEZ, MANUEL LUIS
Drift
Picador
Robert, 16, on the road west to LA

MARTINEZ, VICTOR
Parrot in the Oven
HarperCollins
Manny's family, friends and foes in Fresno

MOHR, NICHOLASA
In Nueva York
Arte Publico
Human stories on the Lower East Side

OSA, NANCY
Cuba 15
Delacorte
Violet, preparing for her quinceañero

PEREZ-BROWN, MARIA
Mamá
Rayo
Latina daughters celebrate their mothers

RICE, DAVID
Crazy Loco
Dial
Nine stories of Mexican American lives

SÁENZ, BENJAMIN ALIRE
Sammy & Juliana in Hollywood
Cinco Puntos
Tough life of a Chicano boy in the 60s

SANTANA, PATRICIA
Motorcycle Ride on the Sea of Tranquility
Univ. of New Mexico
Yolanda and her Mexican American family

SANTIAGO, ESMERALDA
Almost a Woman
Perseus
Finding her identity in Brooklyn

SOTO, GARY
*Help Wanted
Harcourt
Stories of teens facing life's weirdness

TRIANA, GABY
*Cubanita
HarperCollins
Eager to escape her overprotective mother

VEGA, MARTA MORENO
When the Spirits Dance Mambo
Three Rivers
Growing up Nuyorican in El Barrio

VILLASEÑOR, VICTOR
Burro Genius
Rayo
From angry teen to bestselling author

U.S.A Coming to America

AHMEDI, FARAH WITH TAMIM ANSARY
*The Story of My Life
Simon Spotlight
A teen's journey from Kabul to Chicago

BITTON-JACKSON, LIVIA
*Hello, America
Simon and Schuster
A Holocaust survivor begins anew in Brooklyn

BIXLER, MARK
*The Lost Boys of Sudan
Univ. of Georgia
Starting over after years on the run

DANTICAT, EDWIDGE
Behind the Mountains
Orchard
Celiane's diary: from Haiti to Brooklyn

DE LA CRUZ, MELISSA
*Fresh Off the Boat
HarperCollins
Finding her place in a snooty school

GALLO, DONALD R., EDITOR
First Crossing
Candlewick
Stories of today's immigrant teens

GIFF, PATRICIA REILLY
Maggie's Door
Wendy Lamb
Nory travels from Ireland with a dream

HALABY, LAILA
West of the Jordan
Beacon
Palestinian girls in America

HO, MINFONG
The Stone Goddess
Orchard
Memories of lost Cambodia

47

BY WALTER MOSLEY
Little, Brown and Company, 2005

The story you are about to read concerns certain events that occurred in the early days of my life. It all happened over a hundred and seventy years ago. For many of you it might sound like a tall tale because I am no older today than I was back there in the year 1832. But this is no whopper I'm telling; it is a story about my boyhood as a slave and my fated encounter with the amazing Tall John from beyond Africa, who could read dreams, fly between galaxies, and make friends with any animal no matter how wild.

There are many things in the world that most people don't know about. For instance, when I was young nobody ever dreamed that there would be radios and televisions and powerful jet planes that could fly across the ocean in only a few hours. But all of those things were possible back then even though nobody knew it.

NA, AN
A Step from Heaven
Front Street
Bridging two worlds; Korea and America

SACHS, MARILYN
*Lost in America
Roaring Brook
A new life for Nicole in NYC after WWII

TELUSHKIN, JOSEPH, RABBI
The Golden Land
Harmony
The story of Jewish immigration

TESTA, MARIA
*Something About America
Candlewick
Poetic thoughts on fleeing Kosova

U.S.A. Black America

ABDUL-JABBAR, KAREEM AND ANTHONY WALTON
Brothers in Arms
Broadway
Black soldiers at the Battle of the Bulge

BERRY, MARY FRANCES
*My Face is Black is True
Knopf
Demanding payment for unpaid labor

BOLDEN, TONYA
*Maritcha
Abrams
Born free in 19th Century New York City

BOYD, HERB, EDITOR
Autobiography of a People
Anchor
Historical truth- 3 centuries, 116 voices

CLINTON, CATHERINE
The Black Soldier
Houghton Mifflin
From 1492 to the present

CROWE, CHRIS
Getting Away with Murder
Phyllis Fogelman Books
The true story of the Emmett Till case

DERAMUS, BETTY
*Forbidden Fruit
Atria
Heartache on the Underground Railroad

DODSON, HOWARD AND SYLVIANE A. DIOUF, COMPILERS AND EDITORS
In Motion
National Geographic
The African-American migration experience

FINLAYSON, REGGIE
We Shall Overcome
Lerner
History of the civil rights movement

HANSEN, JOYCE AND GARY MCGOWAN
Freedom Roads
Cricket
Searching for the Underground Railroad

HINMAN, BONNIE
*A Stranger in My Own House
Morgan Reynolds
W.E.B. DuBois: writer, speaker, activist

HORTON, JAMES OLIVER AND LOIS E. HORTON
*Slavery and the Making of America
Oxford Univ. Pr.
History of the peculiar institution

HOUSTON, JULIAN
*New Boy
Houghton Mifflin
Rob-outsider in an all-white prep school

HUDSON, WADE
Powerful Words
Scholastic Nonfiction
From Benjamin Banneker to Lauryn Hill

JEROME, FRED AND RODGER TAYLOR
*Einstein on Race and Racism
Rutgers Univ. Pr.
Correcting historical amnesia

KATZ, WILLIAM LOREN
Black Pioneers
Atheneum
Settlers and freedom fighters

LANDAU, ELAINE
Slave Narratives
Watts
Memoirs of those formerly in bondage

MCKISSACK, PATRICIA C. AND FREDRICK L. MCKISSACK
Black Hands, White Sails
Scholastic
Contributions to the whaling industry

MCWORTHER, DIANE
A Dream of Freedom
Scholastic Nonfiction
The pursuit of equality, 1954-1968

MOSLEY, WALTER
*47
Little, Brown
Slave embroiled in a supernatural battle

MYERS, WALTER DEAN AND CHRISTOPHER MYERS
Blues Journey
Holiday House
A father and son's call and response

NELSON, MARILYN WITH ILLUSTRATIONS BY PHILIPPE LARDY
*A Wreath for Emmett Till
Houghton Mifflin
Poems of remembrance and injustice

ROCHELLE, BELINDA
Words with Wings
HarperCollins
A treasury of poetry and art

SHABAZZ, ILYASAH
Growing Up X
One World
A daughter of Malcolm Shabazz speaks

A Wreath for Emmett Till

**BY MARILYN NELSON
WITH ILLUSTRATIONS
BY PHILIPPE LARDY**
Houghton Mifflin Company

Emmett Till's name still catches in my throat,/

like syllables waylaid in a stutterer's mouth./

A fourteen-year-old stutterer, in the South/

to visit relatives and to be taught/

the family's ways. His mother had finally bought/

that White Sox cap; she'd made him swear an oath/

to be careful around white folks. She'd told him the truth/

of many a Mississippi anecdote:/

Some white folks have blind souls. In his suitcase/

she'd packed dungarees, T-shirts, under-wear,/

and comic books. She'd given him a note/

for the conductor, waved to his chubby face,/

wondered if he'd remember to brush his hair./

Her only child. A body left to bloat./

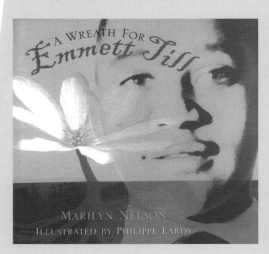

Children of the Great Depression

RUSSELL FREEDMAN
Clarion, 2005

As the nation's First Lady, Mrs. Roosevelt received thousands of letters from the Depression's youngest victims—poor children and teenagers who told her about their problems and often asked for her help. They requested small personal loans so they could stay in school ("I solemnly pledge to pay you back within 2 yrs"); asked for clothing they would not be ashamed to wear ("it just makes my heart ache to know that I can't even afford to dress decent"); wished for holiday gifts their families could not afford ("my poor mother will not be able to get my little sister and brother a doll or toy for Christmas so if your little grandchildren have any little things from last year I will be thankful to see you send them to us").

WEISS, JERRY AND HELEN S. WEISS, EDITORS
Big City Cool
Persea
14 stories of urban American youth

U.S.A. The New Nation

ARONSON, MARC
*The Real Revolution
Clarion
A global view of our independence

BLACKWOOD, GARY
The Year of the Hangman
Dutton
Imagining if Americans lost the war

BOBER, NATALIE S.
Countdown to Independence
Atheneum
A chronology of the years 1760-1776

COX, CLINTON
Come All You Brave Soldiers
Scholastic
5000 Blacks in the Continental Army

FERRIE, RICHARD
The World Turned Upside Down
Holiday House
Washington's victory at Yorktown

FLEMING, CANDACE
Ben Franklin's Almanac
Atheneum
His countless accomplishments

GARLAND SHERRY
In the Shadow of the Alamo
Harcourt
Lorenzo, fighting for the honor of Mexico

HIRSCHFELDER, ARLENE B.
Photo Odyssey
Clarion
Documenting trails blazed to the Pacific

JURMAIN, SUZANNE
*The Forbidden Schoolhouse
Houghton Mifflin
Where African American girls studied

LAVENDER, WILLIAM
Just Jane
Harcourt
A war with loyalties and emotions

MARRIN, ALBERT
George Washington and the Founding of a Nation
Dutton
Farmer, general, president, slaveholder

MILLER, BRANDON MARIE
*Declaring Independence
Lerner
How war affected soldiers and civilians

PEARSALL, SHELLEY
*Crooked River
Random House
An Indian captive facing frontier justice

RINALDI, ANN
Taking Liberty
Simon & Schuster
Oney, enslaved in a presidential home

ST. GEORGE, JUDITH
John and Abigail Adams
Holiday House
President and First Lady, a strong love

WOLF, ALLAN
New Found Land
Candlewick
Imagining the journey of Lewis and Clark

U.S.A. The Civil War and After

BOLDEN, TONYA
*Cause
Knopf
Massive changes after the war

DOUGLASS, FREDERICK
Narrative of the Life of Frederick Douglass, an American Slave
Harvard
As slave and abolitionist

ELLIOTT, L. M.
Annie, Between the States
Katherine Tegen
A patriot of the Confederacy finds love

GIBLIN, JAMES CROSS
*Good Brother, Bad Brother
Clarion
The Booths: one an actor, one an assassin

HAHN, MARY DOWNING
Hear the Wind Blow
Clarion
At 13, fending for himself and his sister

HANSEN, JOYCE
Bury Me Not in a Land of Slaves
Watts
Former slaves' lives during Reconstruction

HOLZER, HAROLD
The President is Shot!
Boyds Mills
The story behind the murder of Lincoln

New York, NY

*new book title

A Time Before Crack

JAMEL SHABAZZ
powerHouse, 2005

The effects of crack would linger on for generations to come.

My generation would sustain the highest rate of casualties from this plague. Sad to say, all of us have known someone who fell victim to its "powerful jaws."

The photographs in this book were taken between 1975 and 1984. They are a visual diary of the encounters I have had with young people throughout New York City. What was most important to me was not so much getting the picture, but having a chance to communicate with them about life and their choices.

After taking the photograph, I would always make it a point to say to them these simple words, "Everything you do today will reflect upon your future," and we would depart, oftentimes never seeing each other again.

This project has granted me the opportunity not only to preserve history, but to also give those who stood in front of my camera the chance to see themselves and their peers, in a time before crack.

JAMEL SHABAZZ
A TIME BEFORE CRACK

ESSAYS BY CHARLIE AHEARN AND TERRENCE JENNINGS
INTRODUCTION BY CLAUDE GRUNITZKY
AFTERWORD BY JAMES "KOE" RODRIGUEZ

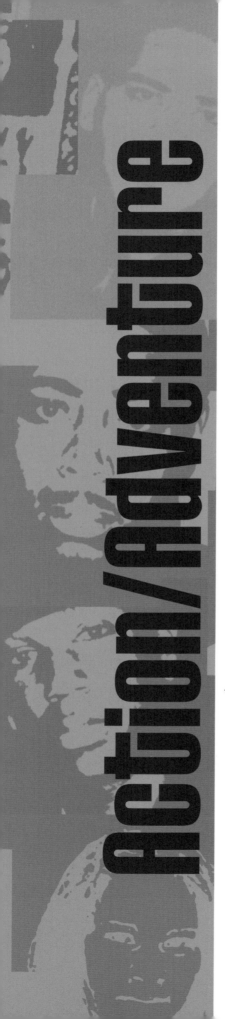

Action/Adventure

Wheels and Wings

BRINGHURST, JOHN
Planes, Jets, & Helicopters
Tab
Great paper airplanes

COLLINS, MARY
Airborne
National Geographic
The Wright Brothers: the first to fly

CROWTHER, NICKY
The Ultimate Mountain Bike Book
Firefly
How to explore all terrains

GIBLIN, JAMES CROSS
Charles A. Lindbergh
Clarion
Pilot and American hero

GRAVELLE, KAREN
***The Driving Book**
Walker
What you need to know

HULLS, JOHN
Rider in the Sky
Crown
An American cowboy's early airplane

KESSEL, ADRIENNE
The World's Strangest Automobiles
Chelsea House
Weird and wonderful cars

MACGREGOR, JEFF
***Sunday Money**
HarperCollins
A year on the road with NASCAR

MILLER, TIMOTHY AND STEVE MILTON
NASCAR Now
Firefly
Everything about stock car racing

MIRRA, DAVE
Mirra Images
ReganBooks
A BMX champion defying gravity

RAMO, JOSHUA COOPER
No Visible Horizon
Simon & Schuster
Thrill and danger of aerial aerobatics

RINARD, JUDITH E.
Book of Flight
Firefly
From the Wright brothers to Mars

WERNER, DOUG
Skateboarder's Start Up
Tracks
Skills, thrills, history, safety

Do-It-Yourself

CALDWELL, BEN
***Fantasy!**
Sterling
Draw knights, warriors, dragons and faeries

CARLE, MEGAN AND JILL CARLE WITH JUDI CARLE
Teens Cook
Ten Speed Press
How to make what you want to eat

CHIARELLO, MARK AND TODD KLEIN
The DC Comics Guide to Coloring and Lettering Comics
Watson-Guptill
Elements that make the story come alive

HAAB, SHERRI
The Hip Handbag Book
Watson-Guptill
Creating the perfect accessory

HANSEN, JIM AND JOHN BRUNS
***Creating Manga Superheroes and Comic Book Characters**
Gramercy
Principles of style, inking, coloring

JANECZKO, PAUL B.
Top Secret
Candlewick
Codes and ciphers: make them, break them

JAYNES, ELA AND DARREN GREENBLATT
Planet Yumthing Do-It-Yourself
Bantam
Projects to make your world sassier

KING, DANIEL
Chess
Kingfisher
Learn to play like a grandmaster

KLEINMAN, KATHRYN
Birthday Cakes
Chronicle
Creating delicious memories

MATTHIESSEN, BARBARA
***Altered Book Collage**
Sterling
Customized pages, original art

MURILLO, KATHY CANO
The Crafty Diva's D.I.Y. Stylebook
Watson-Guptill
Easy-to-do cool creations

OKEY, SHANNON
***Knitgrrl**
Watson-Guptill
Not your grandmother's projects

OLAKSEN, KATHERINE, ELIZABETH MACCRELLISH AND MARGARET M. DONAHUE
***Dorm Room Feng Shui**
Storey
Ditch the clutter, less is more

PRINS, M.D.
***Paper Galaxy**
Sterling
Out-of-this world projects to cut, fold and paste

SCHEUNEMANN, PAM
***Cool Clay Projects**
ABDO
Create colorful gifts

SCHWARTZ, ELLEN
I Love Yoga
Tundra
Breathe, move, relax

SECKEL, AL
The Great Book of Optical Illusions
Firefly
When your eyes trick your brain

WARRICK, LEANNE
Chillin' Trix for Cool Chix
Watson-Guptill
A boredom busting guide

Sports

ANDERSON, LARS AND CHAD MILLMAN
Pickup Artists
Verso
American street basketball

ARON, PAUL
Did Babe Ruth Call His Shot?
Wiley
Baseball mysteries unfolded and solved

BERMAN, LEN
And Nobody Got Hurt
Little, Brown
Ridiculous, unbelievable, phenomenal feats

BURWELL, BRYAN
At the Buzzer
Doubleday
Greatest moments in NBA history

BUXTON, TED
Soccer Skills
Firefly
Drills on every aspect of match play

CHÂTAIGNEAU, GÉRARD AND STEVE MILTON
Figure Skating Now, 2nd edition
Firefly
Pushing the limits of beauty and speed

COFFEY, MICHAEL
27 Men Out
Atria
Baseball's perfect games

DAVIS, JAMES WITH PHOTOGRAPHS BY SKIN PHILLIPS
Skateboarding is Not a Crime
Firefly
A pastime, a lifestyle, a reason, a craze

DIXON, RAMON "TRU" AND DAVID AROMATORIO
How Far Do You Wanna Go?
New Horizon
Inner city baseball champs

GENTILE, DEREK
Smooth Moves
Black Dog & Leventhal
Juking, jamming, hooking and slamming

GOODWIN, JOY
The Second Mark
Simon & Schuster
Battle for Olympic gold in pair skating

HAWK, TONY
Between Boardslides and Burnout.
ReganBooks
Superstar skateboarder tours the world

HUEBNER, MARK AND BRAD WILSON
Sports Bloopers
Firefly
All-star flubs and fumbles

KRASNER, STEVEN
Play Ball Like the Pros
Peachtree
Tips from baseball stars

LAKE, SANOE WITH STEVEN JARRETT
Surfer Girl
Little, Brown
Boards, body image, boys and more

LANNIN, JOANNE
A History of Basketball for Girls and Women
Lerner
Passion, skill, intensity, controversy

LEIKER, KEN AND MARK VANCIL, EDITORS
Unscripted
Pocket
Inside the ring with the WWE

LEWIS, MICHAEL
Coach
Norton
Courage found in a mentor's harsh words

LIBERMAN, NOAH
Glove Affairs
Triumph
Baseball's most valuable piece of equipment

MACY, SUE AND JANE GOTTESMAN
Play Like a Girl
Holt
Celebration of women in sports

MARTINDALE, WIGHT, JR.
Inside the Cage
Simon Spotlight
West 4th: the last urban b-ball bastion

MCDANIELS , PELLOM, III
So You Want to be a Pro?
Addax
Do you have what it takes to succeed?

NACE, DON
Bowling for Beginners
Sterling
How to knock down those pins

O'CONNOR, IAN
The Jump
Rodale
Sebastian Telfair's rise to fame

PORTER, DAVID
Winning Gymnastics for Girls
Facts on File
All the skills and how to master them

RIPKEN, CAL, JR. AND BILL RIPKEN WITH LARRY BURKE
Play Baseball the Ripken Way
Random House
Illustrated guide to the fundamentals

STEEN, SANDRA AND SUSAN STEEN
Take It to the Hoop
Twenty-First Century
100 years of women's basketball

SWISSLER, BECKY
Winning Lacrosse for Girls
Facts on File
How to excel at this high-speed sport

TOMLINSON, JOE WITH ED LEIGH
Extreme Sports
Firefly
Attitude, individuality, no limits

WILSON, LESLIE
The Ultimate Guide to Cheerleading
Three Rivers
Stunts, jumps and chants

Athletes

ARMSTRONG, LANCE WITH SALLY JENKINS
Every Second Counts
Broadway
Tour de France winner, cancer survivor

COFFEY, WAYNE
Winning Sounds Like This
Crown
Women's basketball at Gallaudet

COX, LYNNE
Swimming to Antarctica
Knopf
Tales of a long-distance swimmer

CROTHERS, TIM AND JOHN GARRITY
Greatest Athletes of the 20th Century
Total/Sports Illustrated
Ali, Jordan, Ruth, and others

DE ANGELIS, GINA
Jackie Robinson
Chelsea House
First black in baseball's major leagues

GOTTLIEB, ANDREW
In the Paint
Hyperion
Tattoos of the NBA and what they signify

JETER, DEREK
Game Day
Crown
What it's like to be a Yankee superstar

Ball Don't Lie

MATT DE LA PEÑA
Delacorte Press, 2005

Dreadlock Man,

with his fierce fists and suspect jump shot, sets his stuff ($1.45 sandals, key to bike lock, extra T-shirt) on the bleachers and holds his hands out for the ball. It's ten in the morning and Lincoln Rec has just opened. Sticky's at the free-throw line working out his routine, while all the regulars come swaggering in. *Come on, little man,* Dreadlock Man says. *Give up the rock.*

Sticky throws an around-the-back, no-look dime. Watches Dreadlock Man rise into the air with his awful form—calves tightening, dreads scattering, eyes poised on the goal—and let go of a sorry-looking line drive. Before he comes back down to the dusty old hardwood, he yells out: *Peanut Butter!* Says it every time he takes a jumper. *Peanut Butter!* That's what he wants everyone to call him, but nobody does.

   When the ball ricochets off the side of the backboard, entirely missing the rim, he says what any man would say: *Hey, yo, Stick, let me get one more.*

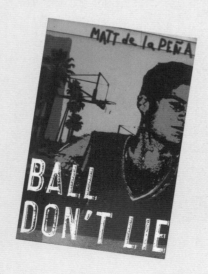

JONES, RYAN
King James
St. Martin's
Basketball phenom, LeBron James

LALLY, RICHARD
Bombers
Crown
Eyewitness accounts of Yankee history

LEIKER, KEN, EDITOR
***Jinxed**
Ballantine
Bizarre baseball rituals revealed

LOUGANIS, GREG WITH ERIC MARCUS
Breaking the Surface
Dutton
Olympic diving champion tells all

MACDONALD, ANDY WITH THERESA FOY DIGERONIMO
Dropping in With Andy Mac
Simon Pulse
Daredevil antics of a pro-skateboarder

MARTIN, MARVIN
Arthur Ashe
Scholastic
His impact on and off the tennis court

OHNO, APOLO ANTON
A Journey
S & S
Olympic gold medal skater, age 20

O'NEAL, SHAQUILLE
Shaq Talks Back
St. Martin's
An honest look at himself and the NBA

RAPOPORT, RON
See How She Runs
Algonquin
Marion Jones: fastest woman in the world

SLATER, KELLY WITH JASON BORTE
Pipe Dreams
ReganBooks
Six-time world champion surfer

SMITH, CHARLES R., JR.
Hoop Kings
Candlewick
Odes to twelve top players

SOSA, SAMMY WITH MARCOS BRETÓN
Sosa
Warner
How he became a record-breaking slugger

STARKS, JOHN WITH DAN MARKOWITZ
John Starks: My Life
Sports Publishing
From tough times to the NBA

STREGE, JOHN
Tiger
Broadway
Golf's first black star

TESSITORE, JOHN
Muhammad Ali
Scholastic
The only three-time heavyweight champ

VANCIL, MARK, EDITOR
***Driven from Within: Michael Jordan**
Atria
The man, the words, the shoes

Action-Packed-Stories

ANDERSON, ERIC CHASE
***Chuck Dugan is AWOL**
Chronicle
Swashbuckling boy hero gone without a trace

AVERETT, EDWARD
***The Rhyming Season**
Clarion
Brenda: drowning her sorrows in the game

DE LA PEÑA, MATT
***Ball Don't Lie**
Random House
Earning his cred on the court & keeping it

FEINSTEIN, JOHN
***Last Shot**
Knopf
Scandal at the college b-ball playoffs

FITZGERALD, DAWN
***Getting in the Game**
Roaring Brook
Joanna elbowing her way onto the ice

HARKRADER, L.D.
***Airball: My Life in Briefs**
Roaring Brook
Shedding his shorts for the court

HIGSON, CHARLIE
***SilverFin**
Miramax
Bond…James Bond-in boarding school

HOBBS, WILL
Leaving Protection
HarperCollins
Finding danger, fishing off Alaska's coast

HOROWITZ, ANTHONY
***Scorpia**
Philomel
Alex Rider: over to the dark side

LAWRENCE, IAIN
***The Convicts**
Delacorte
Convicted of murder, adrift on a prison boat

LIPSYTE, ROBERT
The Contender
HarperCollins
Using boxing to survive

MOWLL, JOSHUA
***Operation Red Jericho**
Candlewick
Investigating a strange disappearance

Driven from Within: Michael Jordan

BY MARK VANCIL, EDITOR
Atria Books, 2005

I WANTED TO PROVE WHAT I COULD DO

When my play started providing me with
rewards, then I wanted to prove I deserved
them. I never felt the desire to rest on
what I had accomplished. I never felt like I
deserved to drive a Bentley when I got my
first contract, or live in a mansion. Those
things might be symbols of success to some
people, but there are a lot of people who
confuse symbols with actual success.

*WHAT'S LEFT AFTER YOU GET ALL THE
MONEY AND BUY THE BEST CAR? THERE'S
NOWHERE TO GO FROM THERE.*

When we won one championship, then I wanted
to win two in a row. When we won two, then I
wanted to win three in a row because Larry and
Magic never won three straight.

NOTHING OF VALUE COMES WITHOUT BEING
EARNED.

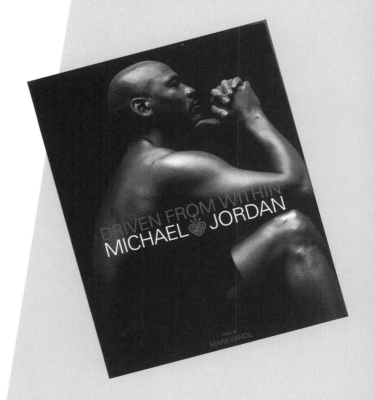

Library Locations

Bronx

Allerton
2740 Barnes Ave.

Baychester
2049 Asch Loop North

Belmont
610 East 186th St.

Bronx Library Center
310 East Kingsbridge Rd.

Castle Hill
947 Castle Hill Ave.

City Island
320 City Island Ave.

Clason's Point
1215 Morrison Ave.

Eastchester
1385 East Gun Hill Rd.

Edenwald
1255 East 233rd St.

Francis Martin
2150 University Ave.

Grand Concourse
155 East 173rd St.

High Bridge
78 West 168th St.

Hunt's Point
877 Southern Blvd.

Jerome Park
118 Eames Place

Kingsbridge
280 West 231st St.

Melrose
910 Morris Ave.

Morrisania
610 East 169th St.

Mosholu
285 East 205th St.

Mott Haven
321 East 140th St.

Parkchester
1985 Westchester Ave.

Pelham Bay
3060 Middletown Rd.

Riverdale
5540 Mosholu Ave.

Sedgwick
1701 Dr. Martin Luther King, Jr. Blvd.

Soundview
660 Soundview Ave.

Spuyten Duyvil
650 West 235th St.

Throg's Neck
3025 Cross Bronx Expressway Extension

Tremont
1866 Washington Ave.

Van Cortlandt
3874 Sedgwick Ave.

Van Nest
2147 Barnes Ave.

Wakefield
4100 Lowerre Place

West Farms
2085 Honeywell Ave.

Westchester Square
2521 Glebe Ave.

Woodlawn Heights
4355 Katonah Ave.

Woodstock
761 East 160th St.

Manhattan

Aguilar
174 East 110th St.

Andrew Heiskell Braille and Talking Book Library
40 West 20th St.

Bloomingdale
150 West 100th St.

Chatham Square
33 East Broadway

Columbus
742 10th Ave.

Countee Cullen
104 West 136th St.

Donnell Library Center
20 West 53rd St.

Early Childhood Resource and Information Center
66 Leroy St.

Epiphany
228 East 23rd St.